SPIRITED MINDS

SPIRITED MINDS

African American
Books for Our Sons
and Our Brothers

Edited by
Archie Givens

Introduction by Gordon Parks

W. W. Norton & Company
New York • London

Managing editors: Desnick & Nelson
Book design: Desnick & Nelson
Writers: Beth Desnick, Erin Sweet, David Jones
Cover illustration by William Raaum

ISBN 0-393-04617-6

W. W. Norton & Company, Inc., 500 Fifth Avenue, New York, N.Y. 10110

This publication has been made possible with the
generous support of the Lilly Endowment Inc.

In memory of my father, Archie Givens, Sr.

To all our sons and brothers.

Contents

Why We Created This Book

When I was quite young, my father impressed upon me the many virtues of reading. Although he never had any formal higher education, he instilled in me a respect for books that has served me throughout my life's work.

Today, far too many young people are missing out on the pleasures and opportunities that come with reading. For some, this is due to a lack of interest; for others, lack of ability. Lack of ability is our greatest concern, but lack of interest is our greatest opportunity because with the right resources and dedication, we can spark interest. And when interest is sparked, learning follows.

That is why we at the Givens Foundation for African American Literature have created *Spirited Minds: African American Books for Our Sons and Our Brothers.* Containing descriptions of more than one hundred carefully selected books, this guide can help prompt an interest in reading, and fan a desire to read even more. All of the books were chosen for their quality as literature, and for the stories they tell about the lives of African American boys and men.

Spirited Minds is for the father, mother, brother, minister, teacher, or grandparent who is looking for books to read to and with young people. In a search for the most engaging works we could find, we looked through hundreds of books and enlisted the help of scholars in African American literature, education specialists, teachers, librarians, and our children. All of these books should be available at your local library or bookstore. If you cannot find a specific selection, consider asking that the book be ordered.

Possessing the ability to read may mean an enriched education, a better job, greater opportunities. But possessing the desire to read means even more: an open door to untold wisdom, adventure, and joy.

Archie Givens

Acknowledgments

So many dedicated people have made this book possible. My first acknowledgment goes to Professor John Wright of the University of Minnesota, whose passion for teaching African American literature inspired us to set our sights high. My thanks to Caroline Knight and Dr. Caroline Majak for their tremendous editorial input, and for expanding our knowledge of young people and reading.

I'd like to thank Anna Foxen for her early work on the book, David Jones for his invaluable research and writing, and Erin Sweet for her further research, writing, and editoral assistance that carried this project to fruition. Thanks also to Miriam Butwin for her wonderful editing, and Anne Knauff for her keen design insights.

My appreciation to Reverend Charles Williams, Colleen Heeter, and Arthur Jordan at the Indiana Black Expo, whose reading project prompted this book; to the Indiana Black Expo reading groups; to Dr. Pat Browne, Florida Harding, Billie Sanders, and Nettie Setter of the Indianapolis School System; to Brandon Meshbesher; and to Sarah Pryor and her son, Clifton Johnson. The enthusiasm of all these people, and so many others, reinforced our determination to make this a book for everyone.

Finally, I'd like to extend my warmest thanks to the Lilly Endowment Inc. and to Willis Bright, Jr., Director of Youth Programs, whose vision and support gave birth to *Spirited Minds.*—A.G.

A Note about Reading Levels

Each of the five chapters in *Spirited Minds* begins with books for very young children, and progresses to books for high school and adult readers. The specific reading levels for each book appear at the end of each book description. In assigning these reading levels, we have analyzed the complexity of words and sentences, as well as subject matter.

Each book falls into one or more of five reading levels: **Picture Books, Grades 1 to 3, Grades 4 to 6, Grades 7 to 9,** and **Grade 10 to Adult.** When a book spans more than one of these reading levels, the skills of the reader should be at the level of the earliest grade stated, but the subject matter will also interest older readers. For instance, a book that is labeled "Grade 7 to Adult," is appropriate for anyone whose reading skills are at least those of a 7th grade student, but the contents of the book will appeal to adults as well.

Many picture books—illustrated books meant to be read to very young children—will also interest older children. The reading levels that follow some of the "Picture Book" designations refer to the grade at which the child will have the skills to read the book independently.

Lastly, when selecting a book to share with another—particularly a young person—it's helpful to look through the book before making a final decision. This valuable step is one of the great joys of sharing books with others.

SPIRITED MINDS

Introduction
by Gordon Parks

Since you have chosen to page through this book, my
faith in you is whole. Somewhere in my past its contents
would have spared me the pain of being lost in my own
darkness; helped me to face my early years with more
confidence, and to confront being born black without fear
of failure.

The schoolbooks issued to my childhood emerge in my
memory filled with heroes—all white. A black author or a
black role model's presence on those pages would have
been startling. No, those books couldn't have recognized
my humblest dreams. Even the newspaper's comic strips,
starring *Maggie and Jiggs* and the likes of the *Katzenjammer
Kids*, ignored my aspirations. The motion pictures I
watched from the "peanut gallery" reserved for blacks also
failed me. Even as a child I sensed something impure in
the way white film heroes like Hoot Gibson and William S.
Hart found glory on the silent screen by murdering
Indians. When black faces appeared—as they seldom
did—their roles were so demeaning, they slaughtered the
dignity my conscience had granted me.

As a young man, I faced so many obstacles in Kansas
that memories of them escape me. Bigotry, discrimination,
and prejudice barked at every turn, and I was without
substantial weapons to fight them off. At fifteen, I found

myself alone in a frigid Minnesota winter—without work, food, or a roof over my head. I was indeed an unlikely candidate for success. Yet I had memories from my past that were particularly fragrant, especially of two people I now consider to be my real heroes—my mother and father. Their words lingered in the distance, waiting for my mind to rejoin their teachings. "If you're going to be somebody," Sarah Parks would say, "you have to want to be somebody. And you have to read about black people who have become somebody." Jackson Parks's advice for taking care of enemies was just as simple and pure: "Waltz around them and do a foxtrot on their backs."

One cold hungry morning, my parents' advice began falling upon me like rain from the depths of my memory. It was as if they had come back from their graves to guide me. Why, I suddenly wondered, had I traveled so many hostile roads without heeding their words? Those dreams I was looking for were still out there somewhere in the distance, still avoiding me.

It took time to absorb my mother and father's advice, but feverishly their hopes were talking to me, urging me to put myself in order; to begin with my head; to begin a search for black writers and heroes. I searched hard and, in one book or another, I found them waiting for me with fire in their tongues, speaking a language that bolstered my hopes. I listened. Plainly, Richard Wright was telling me that a great shadow was moving steadily across the land; that the spirit of the black man was in that shadow— moving it along. Other black writers and poets emerged, fulfilling Wright's words. Langston Hughes, W.E.B. Du Bois, and Arna Bontemps moved in to expand my vision. Then came Ralph Ellison, speaking of the invisibility of blacks in the eyes of whites, and James Baldwin, warning me about the *Fire Next Time.* Before long I was neck-deep in black literature. Indeed, it was a pleasant surprise to learn that black blood flowed in the veins of Alexander Pushkin, Russia's famed poet. Now, in this book, you'll find many other writers with offerings that fill gaps where nothing had been.

Eventually, I would choose to confront those forces of evil with the weapons that had been denied me—reading, self-confidence, courage, and working hard at whatever might bring my life fulfillment. The air was still thick with depression, with the bitterness of those early years, but now there was also hope to help thwart the despair of my youth.

"Life is precious, Pedro. Make the most of it." These were my brother's final words to me moments before he died. And during the years that passed I came to treasure them more and more. They made me ask these questions of myself that I now put to black youth, women, and men. What have you come upon this earth to do? What are the goals you aspire to, the dreams you long for? Have you started putting yourself in order—starting with your head? You owe so much to yourself, to those close to you, and to others who could look up to you someday. To meet this challenge, your knowledge of literature—especially that akin to your African heritage—should be as spotless as your favorite Sunday clothes.

Now, looking back on what helped me most, I see the answer in one word—reading. Without it I would have remained in darkness—without a solid approach to photography, motion pictures, poetry, painting, or music. Certainly my eighteen books would not have appeared. In simple terms, I put what I learned from literature to work. And I allowed these fundamental lessons to work overtime. With them came some additional knowledge that served me well: what I gained from reading good authors of all colors, and from not limiting the possibilities for my own expansion with concern only for my blackness. My thoughts and literary efforts are aimed toward humanity as a whole; toward a heart in Russia or Sweden as well as one in Harlem or Africa. Universality is the key to the door of understanding. That door is what life is all about.

I often think back to Miss MacClintock, a white high school teacher who advised us black students against going to college. "It's a waste of your parents' money," she would say. "You will wind up being porters and maids." I didn't finish high school, but just recently I dedicated my twenty-ninth doctorate to Miss MacClintock. How wonderful if she could have been present to watch me receive it.

So justify my faith in you—read, read, and read. Let those who expect failure from you have a talk with your success. With that done, you can look in the mirror and finally smile at yourself.

Autobiographies
and
Biographies

Coming Home: From the Life of Langston Hughes
(1994)
Written and illustrated by Floyd Cooper
Unpaged

Floyd Cooper brings Langston Hughes's sometimes
lonely childhood alive with thoughtful description and
glowing illustrations, rich in color. Like so many children
today, young Langston kept dreaming of a day when he
would have a home with his mother and father, who were
separated. Hughes spent much of his childhood with his
grandmother, and although she didn't provide the home
he dreamed of, she was an important influence on the
young boy, reading to him and filling his young mind with
the stories of family heroes, including John Mercer
Langston, the country's first African American congress-
man. His grandmother also spoke of her own heroic past,
when she aided runaway slaves as part of the Underground
Railroad. Hughes was a quiet boy, always listening and
dreaming, but as he entered his teens, he started telling
stories and writing poetry. *Coming Home* describes the
boyhood of one of the most celebrated writers in American
history. A gem of a book.

Picture Book, Grades 4 to 6

Alvin Ailey

(1993)

Andrea Davis Pinkney. Illustrations by Brian Pinkney

Unpaged

A s a dancer, Alvin Ailey blazed new paths for African American artists. This picture-book biography describes Ailey's childhood dreams of dancing and his rise to fame as those dreams came true. As a child, Ailey sneaked into a dance theater to watch the performers, and fell in love with modern dance. He studied dance for years, until it became his voice for storytelling. In the 1950s, Ailey started his own dance company and helped to integrate the dance world. Often looking to the blues and gospel music for inspiration, he brought to the stage stories and images drawn from his own cultural experiences. Today, though Ailey is no longer alive, the company he started still thrives. The beauty of the dance world is evident in the big, colorful illustrations on these pages. *Alvin Ailey* is a thoughtful story that all young readers will enjoy.

Picture Book, Grades 4 to 6

I Am Somebody! A Biography of Jesse Jackson

(1992)
James Haskins
112 pages; illustrations

This straightforward biography takes its title from one of the many captivating speeches Jesse Jackson has made during his career as a minister, civil rights activist, politician, and more. In the speech, Jackson proclaimed, "I may be poor, but I am somebody!" The same air of confidence runs through Jackson's entire life. In high school and college, Jackson was a star athlete and a very good student. It was during those years that he became involved in the civil rights movement. Jackson's ambition and determination brought him in close contact with Dr. Martin Luther King, Jr., from whom he drew tremendous inspiration. Since then, Jackson has continued to fight for justice, starting organizations such as Operation Push and the Rainbow Coalition. Also described are Jackson's two important runs for president of the United States in 1984 and 1988. This biography provides a clear message to young people that nothing should limit their dreams.

Grades 4 to 9

Marcus Garvey

(1988)

Mary Lawler. Introduction by Coretta Scott King

110 pages; illustrations

his biography explores the achievements and dreams of Marcus Garvey, and the controversies that swirled around this popular black leader during and after World War I. Black nationalism often traces its roots to Garvey, a Jamaican-born leader who vigorously challenged antiblack prejudice. Garvey moved to New York in 1916, and began promoting his ideas on Harlem street corners, where he talked about racial pride and black solidarity to passersby.

Within two years, Garvey had succeeded in building to international stature the Universal Negro Improvement Association, which he had first established in Jamaica in 1914. He also published his own newspaper, using every means he could to reach out to African Americans. Although he is best known for starting the Back to Africa movement, this biography provides a broader picture of the legendary leader. Filled with interesting photographs, *Marcus Garvey* is an excellent choice for an overview of an unforgettable black leader whose influence runs deep.

Grades 4 to 9

Jazz: My Music, My People

(1994)

Written and illustrated by Morgan Monceaux.
Foreword by Wynton Marsalis
62 pages

J*azz: My Music, My People* is a vibrant, intimate tribute
to the men and women of the jazz world. Writer, painter,
and singer Morgan Monceaux presents readers with short,
storylike biographies of important figures in jazz—from
Buddy Bolden, credited with starting the first jazz band in
the 1890s, to more recent musical pioneers like Charles
Mingus and John Coltrane. Many of the biographies begin
with a personal look at the musician's impact on
Monceaux's life. His mother was a jazz singer herself; she is
the last performer featured in this book.

Readers will be drawn to the many spirited illustrations,
created by the author. Monceaux pairs each biography with
a portrait of the jazz artist, drenched in color and energy.
For the curious reader, there is additional information
about the artists scribbled in the backgrounds of the
paintings. This dazzling, informative book will thrill young
people and adults alike as it asks readers to think about
how music and art interact with their own lives.

Grade 4 to Adult

Narrative of the Life of Frederick Douglass, an American Slave, Written by Himself

(1849)

Frederick Douglass. Preface signed by
William Lloyd Garrison

125 pages

F rederick Douglass' extraordinary autobiography is among the best-known firsthand views of slavery. The power of his writing is still striking today, nearly 150 years after the book was first published. Modern readers are angered and horrified by the treatment Douglass and others he knew received as slaves: the beatings, the separation from family, and the cruelty of overseers whose job was to insure that the human "property" produced to capacity. Though deeply disturbing, Douglass' account is a key chapter in American history and one we should all read. His elegant and authoritative voice reminds us of the progress that has been made and that which is yet to come. Simply told in straightforward, yet highly moving language, *Narrative of the Life of Frederick Douglass* is an amazing account of suffering and triumph.

Grade 7 to Adult

Creative Fire

(1994)
Editors of Time-Life Books
256 pages; illustrations

reative Fire is a beautiful book with an ambitious goal: to document African American achievements in the arts, particularly film, music, literature, and the visual arts. The book is divided into these four areas of creativity, each featuring pictures, photographs, stories, and other details about a stellar group of African American artists. Filmmaker Oscar Micheaux, trumpeter Dizzy Gillespie, playwright August Wilson, and painter Bill Traylor are just a few of the artists highlighted in this colorful book. The book's lively design is one more factor that makes it a fabulous introduction to some of the most talented artists in American history.

Grade 7 to Adult

W.E.B. Du Bois: A Biography
(1972)
Virginia Hamilton
218 pages

Virginia Hamilton brings her characteristic skill and zest to the realm of biography in this warm book detailing the life of W.E.B. Du Bois. She describes Du Bois's childhood in a small Massachusetts town in the 1870s, and how his extraordinary intelligence and ambition earned him a scholarship to Fisk University. His studies there, and later at Harvard and other universities, prepared him for his tremendous achievement as an adult. As a founder of the NAACP and editor of the respected African American magazine, *The Crisis,* Du Bois was a prominent voice for African Americans in the early years of the twentieth century. *W.E.B. Du Bois* is a great introduction to an elegant and influential man who became a major figure in African American history, by an author who has a well-deserved reputation for excellence.

Grade 7 to Adult

The Big Sea: An Autobiography

(1940)

Langston Hughes

335 pages

T*he Big Sea* is a humble, humorous look at the youth and early career of Harlem's best-known writer, the fascinating Langston Hughes. The author covers a lot of territory in this book—from childhood memories to his rise to prominence as a poet during the Harlem Renaissance of the 1920s. Hughes also highlights his travels—first as a teenager, as he and his father journeyed to Mexico, and later in his twenties, when he sailed to Africa, Europe, and other places as a crew member on freighter ships. This autobiography is rich in the musical language that has helped to extend Hughes's fame far beyond his time. A pleasure to read, *The Big Sea* is a long, amazing story full of the adventures, mishaps, and glories of young adulthood, as experienced by one of the most respected American writers of the twentieth century.

Grade 7 to Adult

*The wind blew so strong that it was as dangerous as
the waves. No work was done on deck, for the wind
could pick a man up and lift him off his feet.*

Langston Hughes
The Big Sea: An Autobiography

Letter from the Birmingham Jail

(1994)

Martin Luther King, Jr. Foreword by Bernice A. King

48 pages

Letter from the Birmingham Jail is an intimate look into the mind of Dr. Martin Luther King, Jr., at a critical moment in the civil rights movement. The renowned minister and civil rights leader wrote this masterful letter of protest from a jail cell in Birmingham, Alabama, where he was arrested during a civil rights demonstration in 1963. The letter responds to a public letter eight southern white ministers had published in the Birmingham newspaper, deploring King's nonviolent campaign against segregation. King's letter is a moving point-by-point refutal of their arguments for segregation. He draws on elements from history and religion, and, perhaps most persuasively, from his own life to prove to America that segregation is an unacceptable horror that can be tolerated no longer. Soon after the initial publication of *Letter from the Birmingham Jail*, support for the civil rights movement swelled. Today, the letter stands as testimony to the brilliance and courage of one of our greatest leaders.

Grade 7 to Adult

Sugar Ray
(1970)

Sugar Ray Robinson and Dave Anderson

376 pages

Sugar Ray Robinson carved an outstanding career out of the sport often called "the sweet science." Success at boxing demands confidence—some would say arrogance—and Sugar Ray combined his one-of-a-kind ring skills with an attitude that helped propel him to stardom. As a child, he met the legendary Joe Louis while the boxer was training in Detroit. Sugar Ray would follow in Louis's footsteps to world championships in boxing. In this book he looks back on his high-living days, seeing himself as "neither saint nor sinner," but instead as a chosen man. This spunky, artfully told autobiography will appeal to a wide audience.

Grade 7 to Adult

Days of Grace: A Memoir

(1993)

Arthur Ashe and Arnold Rampersad

317 pages

rthur Ashe rose to stardom in tennis, and thus became one of the first African American athletes to break the color barrier in the sport. In this memoir, Ashe describes high points of his career, including his 1975 victory over Jimmy Connors at Wimbledon, as well as painful episodes such as the public furor over his diagnosis with AIDS. Right down to his death in 1993, Ashe remained a political activist, engaged in both national and international causes. The frankness of his memoir offers readers a unique political statement from a caring and thoughtful man. Ashe speaks in detail about the difficulties of growing up in an atmosphere of explicit racial segregation, and he is equally direct in confronting other barriers to black achievement in later eras. This book is a revealing commentary by a brave champion in the world of sports.

Grade 10 to Adult

The Fire Next Time

(1963)

James Baldwin

120 pages

In *The Fire Next Time,* James Baldwin spares few targets as he thoughtfully examines America's record on racism, confronting topics as diverse as Christianity, capitalism, black nationalism, and white backlash. Baldwin draws on his own experiences in the two moving essays that make up this book. The first is a letter he wrote to his nephew on the hundredth anniversary of the Emancipation; the second, a longer, more detailed look at matters of race. Throughout the book, Baldwin combines strong emotion with vivid imagery to highlight his point that we all must work to "end the racial nightmare." *The Fire Next Time,* released at the peak of the civil rights era, received rave reviews. It remains a challenging and important book in our own time.

Grade 10 to Adult

The Autobiography of LeRoi Jones

(1984)

Imamu Amiri Baraka (formerly LeRoi Jones)

329 pages

Bold, unapologetic, and openly political—these words describe not just Amiri Baraka, but also his writing. This detailed, free-wheeling autobiography takes readers through Baraka's early days of bohemian rebellion, to his later involvement with black nationalism and other movements. Baraka, born LeRoi Jones, first gained popularity with the Beat Generation poets in New York City, but as the Black Arts Movement began to take hold, his writing focused almost entirely on emotions and images associated with his African American heritage.

Baraka has constantly challenged traditional ideas about the style, subject, and content of literature. No matter what he is writing about, Baraka has sought to unfold the mysteries of blackness and to celebrate the beauty and wonder of the African personality. This is an extraordinary tale by a writer who has made a powerful contribution to the body of African American literature.

Grade 10 to Adult

Soledad Brother: The Prison Letters of George Jackson
(1970)
George Jackson. Introduction by Jean Genet
330 pages

This collection of George Jackson's letters from prison overflows with anger and intelligence. His letters capture the intense feelings of rebellion that surged in prisons during the peak era of black nationalism in the late 1960s. Jackson was no stranger to a jail cell when he was convicted of the robbery that landed him in Soledad Prison. He pleaded guilty to the offense with the understanding that he would receive a light, county jail sentence, but he remained at Soledad until his death in 1971 during a prison uprising. While there, Jackson read and wrote extensively, describing his life in prison and eloquently expressing his anger at racist white America. *Soledad Brother* remains relevant today, when African American men are still vastly over-represented in the American prison system.

Grade 10 to Adult

The Autobiography of Malcolm X

(1965)

Malcolm X and Alex Haley, who also wrote the epilogue.
Introduction by M.S. Handler

455 pages

This intensely personal autobiography was completed shortly before Malcolm X was gunned down in 1965. It is both a history of the man and a vivid expression of his passion for justice and action. Early in Malcolm X's life, his father, a follower of Marcus Garvey, was murdered by white supremacists in Malcolm's hometown of Omaha. His mother worked hard to instill a sense of pride in young Malcolm, who was told early in his school years that it made no sense for a "Negro" to dream of being a lawyer— it just wasn't possible. Malcolm X learned about the Nation of Islam in prison and eventually became an articulate spokesman for the group. His outspoken advocacy of black empowerment, his fall from favor with the Nation of Islam, and his tragic murder leave much for later generations to reflect upon. For the dedicated reader, this book will provide a captivating glimpse into the mind of a hero.

Grade 10 to Adult

*I've never been one for inaction. Everything I've ever
felt strongly about, I've done something about.*

Malcolm X
The Autobiography of Malcolm X

Makes Me Wanna Holler: A Young Black Man in America

(1994)
Nathan McCall
416 pages

Emotional and intense, *Makes Me Wanna Holler* is a detailed autobiographical coming-of-age story that will hold readers spellbound. A very bright child, Nathan McCall always excelled in school until he reached junior high and his priorities shifted drastically—proving his masculinity at any cost became more important than proving his intellect. Although he put very little effort into his studies, McCall managed to graduate from high school and gain admittance to a nearby college. At the same time, his involvement in drugs, guns, and crime continued to grow until it led to his imprisonment on an armed robbery charge. McCall chronicles his journey to his present occupation; he is now a writer for the *Washington Post.* This autobiography is more than a brutally honest look back on a lifestyle many teenagers today will relate to; it is also an articulate examination of the cultural forces that make adolescence such a dangerous time for many black youth.

Grade 10 to Adult

No Free Ride: From the Mean Streets to the Mainstream

(1996)

Kweisi Mfume and Ron Stodghill II

373 pages; illustrations

No Free Ride is a frank and intimate portrait of a leader. Kweisi Mfume explores his life with seasoned wisdom, writing about a childhood scarred by an abusive stepfather, but also of the other men who gave him the self-confidence and determination that he would carry with him throughout life. Mfume's mother died when he was only sixteen years old. Left to fend for himself, he fell prey to the excitement, easy money, and respect that a life on the street offered him. By the age of twenty-two, he had fathered five sons out of wedlock and had little income with which to support them. It was not long until a moment of epiphany changed his life—forever. Mfume details his transition from street thug to college student, then to radio disc jockey and later, Baltimore City Council member. His journey also led to Congress, where he eventually headed the Congressional Black Caucus. Today, Mfume heads the NAACP. Written with grace and honesty, his story is an inspiration.

Grade 10 to Adult

A Choice of Weapons
(1966)
Gordon Parks
274 pages

In this gripping autobiography, Gordon Parks explores his journey to manhood. Once a cold, hungry sixteen-year-old left to survive on his own during a brutal Minnesota winter, Parks eventually found fame as a writer, musician, photographer, and filmmaker. As a young man, Parks began his fight to educate himself and, in his words, "to prove my worth." Teaching himself photography with a secondhand camera, Parks began to document the poverty among African Americans on Chicago's South Side and created the photographs that helped launch his career as a photographer for *Life* magazine.

A Choice of Weapons describes how Parks managed to overcome poverty and bigotry by using the weapons given him by "a mother who placed love, dignity, and hard work over hatred." This autobiography is a compelling, lively, inspirational book by a man who has succeeded in new artistic endeavors again and again.

Grade 10 to Adult

Four Lives in the Bebop Business

(1966)

A.B. Spellman

241 pages

A B. Spellman provides fascinating insights into the evolution of modern jazz through his look at the lives and artistry of four innovative composer/musicians who came on the scene during the height of the bebop era. Written largely in the words of the artists and their contemporaries, these engaging biographies provide a unique perspective on the early careers of Cecil Taylor, Ornette Coleman, and Jackie McLean, who all went on to achieve critical acclaim, and Herbie Nichols, whose career was cut short by illness before he could receive any significant recognition for his work. Each artist faced many obstacles in his attempts to bring his music to the public. The artists' challenging compositional and musical styles, as well as their eccentric personalities, often provoked puzzled if not negative responses from club owners, critics, fellow musicians, and their audiences. Spellman's book portrays a critical time in the history of jazz, and exemplifies how the genius of innovation is often rejected initially, only to be freely pirated by others in later years.

Grade 10 to Adult

Brothers and Keepers

(1984)
John Edgar Wideman
243 pages

T his book presents readers with an intriguing premise:
in one family, two brothers grow up—one becomes a
college professor and a writer, while the other ends up
imprisoned for robbery and murder. In *Brothers and Keepers*,
author John Wideman asks: why the difference? This is a
difficult question to answer under any circumstances, but
to complicate matters further, Wideman is examining his
own family. Prison interviews with Wideman's brother
Robby and letters between the brothers provide the raw
material for this autobiographical book. Wideman's
extremely personal look at family dynamics and sibling
relationships gives this book its intensity. Complex and
challenging, yet very readable, *Brothers and Keepers* promises
to captivate readers with its portrait of two brothers—both
very intelligent—whose lives took very different paths.

Grade 10 to Adult

Black Boy: A Record of Childhood and Youth

(1945)
Richard Wright
228 pages

B*lack Boy* traces Richard Wright's development as a writer in the most difficult circumstances imaginable. A history of Wright's early years, the book describes his experiences growing up in the Deep South just after the turn of the century, and continues through his young adult years in the North. Denial of equal education and jobs, exclusion from entire neighborhoods, and violence at the hands of whites were routine. Wright battles segregation, seething prejudice, and violence in his lifelong struggle for self-awareness. When this book was first published in 1945, it contained only half of what Wright had written, because his publisher feared censorship. A new, restored version of the book as Wright wished it to be read was published in 1991, and is highly recommended. *Black Boy* remains a vital commentary on racism and the drive to overcome obstacles, as well as a riveting autobiography by a brilliant author.

Grade 10 to Adult

Drama

Escape to Freedom: A Play about Young Frederick Douglass

(1976)

Ossie Davis

90 pages

O ssie Davis captures the childhood of Frederick Douglass with energy and emotion in this play aimed at young people. *Escape to Freedom* begins with the hero's birth, and takes readers up to his daring escape from slavery. Using a cast of just seven actors, the play explores important moments for young Frederick, including the dramatic story of how he learned to read and write; how he attempted to share with other slaves every shred of knowledge he picked up; and his legendary victory over the "slave breaker," Covey. *Escape to Freedom* is a very simple play designed to introduce children not just to Frederick Douglass, but to the magic of drama as well.

Grade 4 to Adult

The Amen Corner: A Play

(1968)

James Baldwin

91 pages

James Baldwin explores the power, the glory, and the hypocrisy of the church in this moving play about a female pastor's fall from grace in the eyes of her Harlem congregation. Margaret Alexander is confronted with disturbing dilemmas as *The Amen Corner* opens: behind her back, the elders of the church are falsely accusing her of swindling the church's money and other misdeeds. The elders say it is time for her to step down from the pulpit. Meanwhile, her home is in disarray. Luke, the musician husband Margaret left so many years ago, has appeared at her door, and he is dying. Her teenage son has anounced he is leaving the church for a life of music. All of these things make Margaret question her faith. In the end, Margaret finds that although she may fall from grace in the congregation's eyes, for the first time in her life she will be able to find peace in her soul. *The Amen Corner* is a tender exploration of religion written by one of the most acclaimed American writers of the twentieth century.

Grade 7 to Adult

A Raisin in the Sun: A Drama in Three Acts

(1959)

Lorraine Hansberry

142 pages

This magnificent play introduces readers to the Youngers—an extended family haunted and tortured by unfulfilled dreams. As the play opens, the Youngers await a $10,000 check in the mail. The check is an insurance settlement arising from the death of Lena Younger's husband. All have their eyes on the money, especially Lena's grown son, Walter Lee, whose plans for investing the money are dubious and risky. Yet, the battle over money is about much more than greed; it is the catalyst for a confrontation about the family members' conflicting and unachieved dreams. *A Raisin in the Sun* was the first play by an African American woman to be produced on Broadway. With intensity and dignity, it captures the dynamics of a family in the midst of a painful crisis.

Grade 7 to Adult

Twilight: Los Angeles, 1992
On the Road: A Search for
American Character
(1994)
Anna Deavere Smith
265 pages; illustrations

Anna Deavere Smith has created a masterpiece out of tragedy: the riots that erupted in Los Angeles after the police officers accused of brutally beating Rodney King were found not guilty. In the emotional aftermath of the violence, Anna Deavere Smith interviewed 200 people— men and women of all races, classes, and occupations. She interviewed gang members, police officers, senators, scholars, and the individuals who were caught up in the riots, like Reginald Denny. Out of these interviews, Smith created a one-woman play. Over fifty of those characterizations are included in this book, each written to reflect the speaking style of the person portrayed. An unusual work of drama, *Twilight: Los Angeles, 1992* is a very emotional and honest look at our times.

Grade 7 to Adult

The Piano Lesson

(1990)

August Wilson

108 pages

As the *The Piano Lesson* begins, Boy Willie Charles considers a very tempting opportunity: whether or not to buy a plot of southern farmland owned by the Sutter family. Long ago, Boy Willie's ancestors were slaves of the Sutter family, but now the passage of time will turn the tables—if Boy Willie can scrape together the money to buy the land. At the center of his money-making strategy is a very valuable, hand-carved parlor piano he and his sister Berniece inherited from their father. Boy Willie wants to sell the piano, which sits in Berniece's Pittsburgh living room collecting dust, but she refuses to even consider it— for her, the family history carved into the piano is too sacred to throw away. This battle between siblings, compli- cated by the appearance in the play of ghosts from an earlier time, raises many questions about the importance of preserving the past.

Grade 7 to Adult

BERNIECE: Money can't buy what that piano cost.
You can't sell your soul for money.

August Wilson
The Piano Lesson

Dutchman and The Slave, Two Plays

(1964)
Imamu Amiri Baraka (formerly LeRoi Jones)
88 pages

Together, the two plays in this book offer a scorching intellectual analysis of race relations in the 1960s. The plays helped earn Amiri Baraka, born LeRoi Jones, a reputation as a provocative writer. Both plays directly address conflicts between races in ways that had never before been portrayed on the stage. *Dutchman* features Clay, an intelligent twenty-year-old African American man. An older white woman, Lula, sits down next to him on the subway and strikes up a conversation. Lula alternates between trying to seduce the young man with sexual innuendos and trying to antagonize him with racial slurs. The play ends in an unexpected display of violence. *The Slave* also features an African American man and a white woman, a divorced couple. The play is set in the midst of a race revolution. Each play met a sea of controversy and, in some places, even censorship. *Dutchman and The Slave* marked the rise of black nationalism in the work of one of America's most daring writers.

Grade 10 to Adult

The Day the Bronx Died
(1996)

Michael Henry Brown

94 pages

A tragic event affecting his teenage son causes a middle-aged African American man to reflect upon his own boyhood in this disturbing and thoughtful play by Michael Henry Brown. Big Mickey takes us back to the Bronx in 1968, recounting the summer of his thirteenth year, when his greatest loves were miming to the sounds of his favorite musical group with his black friend, Alexander, and playing baseball with his Jewish friend, Billy. In the play, these harmless pleasures are soon corrupted by the realities of the times. Increasingly tense race relations, climaxing with the death of Dr. Martin Luther King, Jr., cause Alexander to condemn Mickey's friendship with Billy. A violent gang's domination of the neighborhood also makes life unsafe for the young teenager who is unwilling to bow to the ringleader. Mickey faces increasing internal conflict as he questions his relationships, and as he struggles to act responsibly and uphold his concept of "the truth." This moving and troubling drama captures the anguish of a boy and man in the midst of crisis.

Grade 10 to Adult

The Darker Face of the Earth:
A Verse Play in Fourteen Scenes

(1994)

Rita Dove. Illustrations by Mark Woolley

140 pages

I n this painfully familiar and yet breathtakingly
innovative play, recent U.S. Poet Laureate Rita Dove takes
an ancient Greek tale—Oedipus the King—and places it in
pre–Civil War South Carolina. According to the ancient
story, the abandoned child Oedipus is doomed to sleep
with his mother and kill his father without knowing who
they are. In *The Darker Face of the Earth*, this story is made
even more complicated by the realities of black-white
sexual relations during slavery. As the play starts out,
Amalia, a young slaveowner, intentionally gets pregnant by
one of her male slaves in order to get back at her husband
for his relations with the female slaves. Her baby is sold
into slavery and seemingly forgotten for twenty years, until
an extremely intelligent and equally rebellious twenty-year-
old slave named Augustus comes to the plantation and
starts spending a great deal of time with Amalia. Rita
Dove's daring retelling of this Greek tragedy retains all of
its original drama and will keep readers riveted.

Grade 10 to Adult

Five Plays

(1963)

Langston Hughes. Introduction by Webster Smalley

258 pages

The five plays in this collection range from the very serious to the extremely silly. The opening play, *Mulatto*, tells the painful story of Bert, a young man whose mother, Cora, is a black housekeeper, and whose father, Thomas Norwood, is a rich white plantation owner. A good balance to this emotional story can be found in another play, appropriately titled *Simply Heavenly*. This play puts one of Hughes's most famous and entertaining characters, Jesse B. Semple, into a dramatic setting where his humor can really shine. The three other plays in this book—a comedy set in 1920s Harlem, *Little Ham*, a gospel-like story of the battle between good and evil called *Tambourines to Glory*, and the complicated drama *Soul Gone Home*—round out this collection. Readers will find *Five Plays* a stunning example of Langston Hughes's incredible skill as a writer.

Grade 10 to Adult

Mule Bone: A Comedy of Negro Life
(1991)
Langston Hughes and Zora Neale Hurston
282 pages

M*ule Bone* is a rollicking comedy drawn from black folklore, in which a ridiculous argument between friends erupts into a controversy that divides a town. When Methodist Jim Weston hits Dave Carter, a Baptist, over the head with a mule bone during a fight about a woman, the town of Eatonville splits into two camps—the Methodists, who of course think Jim should be pardoned, and the Baptists, who are in favor of expelling him from the town.

Langston Hughes and Zora Neale Hurston were both talented young literary stars of the Harlem Renaissance when they wrote this play together over sixty-five years ago. Their mysterious dispute over who actually wrote the play kept it from being performed or published during either writer's lifetime. Included in this book are other writings about the authors' dispute, some of which might amuse readers as much as the play itself. *Mule Bone* is not only a clever take on the mishaps of jealousy, but also on the egos of two of the most famous writers of American literature.

Grade 10 to Adult

The National Black Drama Anthology: Eleven Plays from America's Leading African American Theaters

(1995)
Edited by Woodie King, Jr.
515 pages

T his collection showcases the vitality and talent to be found in African American drama written and produced today. The eleven plays are diverse in subject and style. Bill Harris's *Robert Johnson: Trick the Devil* gives voice to an important figure of the blues era, while Denise Nichols's *Buses* is a tribute to the spirit of Rosa Parks, and C. Bernard Jackson's *Iago* draws on Shakespeare for inspiration. *Tod, the Boy Tod*, by Talvin Wilks, is a dreamlike play described as a "Rap Rock Ritual Dance Theatre piece." Also supplied are profiles of the theaters that nourished these plays; all are black-controlled and located in various inner cities. This anthology is a great introduction to the African American theater scene today, sure to inspire and inform anyone with an interest in drama.

Grade 10 to Adult

Novels
and
Short Stories

The Leaving Morning

(1992)

Angela Johnson. Illustrations by David Soman

Unpaged

This simple, touching picture book explores a young boy's views about his family's move out of their apartment to a new place. As the children in this book point out, moving can be difficult—it means saying goodbye to neighbors, friends, and relatives, not to mention a familiar environment. Angela Johnson conveys with sensitivity the feelings of uncertainty and apprehension that children often experience in a move. She also shows young readers that moving isn't all sadness: it can also mean excitement and special attention from thoughtful neighbors. The warm watercolor illustrations brilliantly capture the changing moods of the children. *The Leaving Morning* is an excellent book to share with a young child, one that offers many avenues for discussion.

Picture Book

My Friend Jacob

(1980)

Lucille Clifton. Illustrations by Thomas DiGrazia

Unpaged

Told from the viewpoint of Sam, an eight-year-old boy, *My Friend Jacob* reminds us that the closest and, often, unexpected friendships can pop up if we don't judge people who are different. Sam is best friends with Jacob, a teenager who lives next door. Though it is not clearly stated anywhere in the book, the illustrations and Jacob's behavior suggest he has a learning disorder. The boys like to play together just like any other set of best friends. Jacob teaches Sam how to play basketball, and Sam helps Jacob remember the things that are difficult for him, like what to buy at the store, and when to safely cross the street. They never tease each other or laugh when one of them makes a mistake. Author Lucille Clifton has a special friend like Jacob and, with this touching book, she reminds children and adults alike of the true meaning of friendship.

Picture Book to Grade 3

Clean Your Room, Harvey Moon!

(1991)

Written and illustrated by Pat Cummings

Unpaged

Author and illustrator Pat Cummings exposes one of childhood's injustices—from the perspective of the child, that is—in this book that will make children and the adults who read it with them laugh out loud. It's Saturday morning and Harvey is plopped in front of the television, waiting for his favorite cartoon to start, when his mother announces he has to clean his room—right away. Cummings brings to life the humor of the story with simple rhyming words that make this book a great choice to read aloud. Large, dynamic illustrations capture Harvey's messy room with bright colors and an attention to detail that make the pictures as fun to look at as the story is to read. *Clean Your Room, Harvey Moon!* is pure fun—the perfect book to share with a young child.

Picture Book to Grade 3

Jamal's Busy Day
(1991)

Wade Hudson. Illustrations by George Ford

Unpaged

I n this charming picture book, Jamal tells readers about an average day in his family's life. Everyone gets up early to go to work. Jamal's dad is an architect who "makes drawings" and his mom is an accountant who "works with numbers." And, as Jamal informs readers, during his own busy day, he does all of these things and more. The way Jamal sees it, he has supervisors just as his parents do, only his are called teachers. He has co-workers, too—his classmates. Jamal lets readers know that going to school every day is serious business, just like a job. His day isn't all work, however. He also plays basketball and reads, so that he can "unwind." And, at the end of the day, Jamal can't wait for the next one to begin. This interesting book, full of bright, full-color illustrations, invites discussion about young readers' own busy days.

Picture Book to Grade 3

Max Found Two Sticks

(1994)

Written and illustrated by Brian Pinkney

Unpaged

The story of Max and his "drumsticks" ties into the rich musical history of African Americans. One day Max just doesn't feel like talking, so he sits on his front steps and watches the sky. When two sturdy twigs fall from a nearby tree, he uses them to play makeshift drums: hatboxes, soda bottles, garbage cans—whatever is handy and makes an interesting sound. The rhythms of the world around him are, as Max discovers, raw materials for the musician's ear. Max also learns that the world is responsive to the call of music, even the homemade rhythms of two twigs on a cleaning bucket. The author's beautiful full-color illustrations add to the wonder of this book. Adults will enjoy sharing Brian Pinkney's magical world of rhythm and music with young children.

Picture Book to Grade 3

Jonathan and His Mommy

(1992)

Irene Smalls. Illustrations by Michael Hays

Unpaged

I rene Smalls dedicates this book to "all the beautiful black men" in her family, setting the tone for this story about a young boy and his mother who like to take walks together. During their strolls, they try zigzag steps, giant steps, and a full run—and they don't care a bit about the looks they get from passersby. The writing captures the rhythm of their steps, and Michael Hays's moving illustrations highlight their loving relationship and reflect the joy of the city on a warm summer day.

Picture Book to Grade 3

Storm in the Night

(1988)

Mary Stolz. Illustrations by Pat Cummings

Unpaged

This picture book explores the creeping fear many children experience whenever a thunderstorm booms and thrashes about, and a young boy's wish to try to hide that fear. The beautiful illustrations painted in deep purples, blues, and greens help create the feeling of a stormy night. When Thomas and his grandfather lose the electricity in their home during a violent thunderstorm, it is the perfect time for a story. Thomas is amused to hear his grandfather talk about his childhood, because the young boy can hardly imagine his grandfather was once his age. Though Thomas claims that the storm doesn't scare him, his grandfather tells how he overcame his own fear of storms with a little help from his dog, Melvin. *Storm in the Night* is a wonderful story about fear, love, and responsibility.

Picture Book to Grade 3

John Henry
(1994)

Julius Lester. Illustrations by Jerry Pinkney

Unpaged

The legend of John Henry will captivate children in this lively, wonderfully written version of the classic folktale. From the moment John Henry is born, he starts growing so fast that his shoulders break right through the roof over his head. From this point on, John Henry uses his incredible strength to help people. The suspense of the tale peaks when John Henry gets in a race with a steam drill to see who can hammer through a mountain first, so railroad tracks can be laid. No one would expect a man to beat a machine, but John Henry is no ordinary man. Jerry Pinkney's masterful, full-color illustrations underscore the beauty of the man and his landscape. Julius Lester's *John Henry* is an unforgettable version of a classic folktale.

Picture Book to Grade 6

The Stories Julian Tells

(1981)

Ann Cameron. Illustrations by Ann Strugnell

71 pages

J ulian tells stories about homemade lemon pudding that "tastes like a night on the sea" and other curiosities in this book featuring an imaginative young boy and his loving family. These six light-hearted and whimsical stories, written from the vantage point of eight-year-old Julian, serve as a model for children to create their own tales of wonder and mischief. All of them stress the importance of family and respect; in "Gloria Who Might Be My Best Friend," one of the most moving stories in the book, Julian befriends a girl even though "people find out and tease you." The black-and-white illustrations help stir the fancy, but it is the simple, amusing writing style that will grab and hold a reader's attention. *The Stories Julian Tells* is a feast for the imagination—perfect for young readers.

Grades 1 to 6

Justin and the Best Biscuits in the World

(1986)

Mildred Pitts Walter. Illustrations by Catherine Stock

122 pages

Ten-year-old Justin is having a tough time as the only man in the house. His mother and sisters expect him to wash dishes, clean his room, and cook for himself, but when he tries and makes a mess, they get angry. Justin thinks cooking and cleaning are "women's work" until he spends a few days alone with his grandfather on the family ranch. There, Grandpa patiently shows Justin how to make a bed and wash dishes and, of course, how to make the best biscuits in the world. Grandpa also teaches him about the family's history. Justin's great-grandfather was also ten when his family risked everything to escape from the South to Missouri, where they settled down and built the ranch. Justin also learns about other black cowboys when he gets to experience a real rodeo. The black-and-white illustrations go well with the crisp writing. This story is a tribute to the patience and love of grandparents everywhere.

Grades 1 to 6

Sidewalk Story

(1971)

Sharon Bell Mathis. Illustrations by Leo Carty

73 pages

W hen Lilly Etta Allen sees her friend Tanya and her family evicted from their apartment because Tanya's mother had to spend the rent money on food, she knows somebody has to stop it. She doesn't understand why the adults in the neighborhood, including her own mother, don't seem willing to fight the injustice before their eyes. Tanya's mother has struggled to raise seven children by herself. She works very hard, but she can't earn enough to keep everyone fed and pay the rent. Where will Tanya and her family go? Lilly Etta wonders. What will happen to all their belongings heaped on the sidewalk?

Sidewalk Story is about the heroic struggle of a nine-year-old who refuses to accept the way the world treats her friend's family. Lilly Etta's dramatic actions force more than one adult to take a close look at what's happening in their community. Large, realistic black-and-white illustrations convey the distinctive urban setting of a story written, says the author, as a tribute to "the strength and beauty" of African American children.

Grades 4 to 6

Chevrolet Saturdays

(1993)

Candy Dawson Boyd

176 pages

F ifth grader Joey Davis feels like he's suddenly arrived in a world where everything that gave him comfort and security has disappeared. His parents have recently divorced and now Joey has to adjust to a stepfather, Mr. Johnson. Joey misses his real father, who is looking for a job in Chicago, thousands of miles from Joey's California home. His new teacher, Mrs. Hamlin, makes Joey's days in school miserable—he knows he is smart enough to be in the gifted class, but she won't let him take the test to qualify for the program. To make matters worse, Joey is being bullied at school. The power of friendship and hard work is tested in this realistic story about ambition and the challenges of the world. *Chevrolet Saturdays* brings together in one inspiring story several difficult modern issues facing many young boys today.

Grades 4 to 9

The Gift-Giver

(1980)

Joyce Hansen

118 pages

Amir is different from the other kids on 163rd Street in the Bronx. For one thing, he isn't concerned about what other children think of him. He doesn't tease anyone, and he doesn't play basketball with the other boys—he just watches. Amir has just transferred to Doris's school, where they are both in the fifth grade. At first, it doesn't seem as if Amir will fit in with the 163rd Street crowd, but his quiet, helpful, wise ways win over everyone. He and Doris become best friends during the school year, and he encourages her not to follow the crowd but to do what her heart tells her. They both have serious problems to deal with in their lives—unemployed parents, gangs, split families—but Doris and Amir find comfort in talking about their troubles and those of their friends. A teacher herself, author Joyce Hansen describes this dramatic and emotional book as "a novel about love and hope." In *The Gift-Giver*, these qualities are presented as the tools for survival.

Grades 4 to 9

The Friendship

(1987)

Mildred D. Taylor. Illustrations by Max Ginsburg

53 pages

T his story raises issues of loyalty, friendship, and racial discord in the American South during the 1930s. Cassie Logan and her brothers have orders to stay away from John Wallace's store, but when a sick neighbor sends them for medicine, they have no choice but to go. At the store, the Logan children witness a confrontation between Tom Bee, an elderly black man, and John Wallace, the white shop-keeper. When Tom Bee refuses to call the storekeeper "Mr. John," he breaks a major unwritten rule of the community: no black person addresses a white man by his first name only. The events witnessed by the children make them aware of the tragic absurdity and injustice of race relations in their community. Brief and easy to read, this novel is powerfully written by an author who can tell a complicated story with clarity and zest.

Grades 4 to 9

The Watsons Go to Birmingham—1963

(1995)

Christopher Paul Curtis

211 pages

he Watsons Go to Birmingham—1963 gives readers an intimate glimpse into the often humorous but sometimes painful world of ten-year-old Kenny Watson, who lives in Flint, Michigan, with his family. Kenny's older brother Byron, at thirteen, has turned into "an official juvenile delinquent" and his parents have decided to take him to live for awhile with his grandmother in Alabama.

Despite everyone's expectations, the trip will turn out to be most difficult for Kenny himself. During the vacation, the young boy has experiences which force him to grapple with the idea of death and to face racism in its most violent form. This story slides from laugh-out-loud humor into wrenching pain, with very little notice. It will enthrall young people as well as adults with its vivid portrayal of a ten-year-old boy's struggle to make sense of a world that sometimes defies meaning.

Grade 4 to Adult

The Sweet Flypaper of Life
(1955)
Roy DeCarava and Langston Hughes
98 pages; illustrations

The Sweet Flypaper of Life highlights the magic and beauty of Harlem with black-and-white photographs by Roy DeCarava and a warm and humorous text by Langston Hughes. Set in the 1950s, this engaging story is told by Sister Mary Bradley. She has been called to heaven by a bicycle messenger from the Lord, but doesn't want to go. She has some good reasons to stay alive: her grandchildren need care, Harlem is a beautiful place that she doesn't want to leave, and she's curious to see if "this integration" will get rid of prejudice. Pictures and story together make a persuasive case for clinging to—and enjoying—the "sweet flypaper of life" at any age. This classic will be enjoyed by adults and young people alike.

Grade 4 to Adult

M.C. Higgins, the Great

(1974)

Virginia Hamilton

278 pages

This novel introduces readers to M.C. Higgins, a young man who spends his summer days watching over his family and their land on Sarah's Mountain. He perches himself upon a bicycle seat he has attached to a forty-foot pole that shoots up from the family graveyard. For M.C.'s father, the pole serves as an unconventional marker for the graves of his relatives.

From his unusual seat high in the air, M.C. can see the beauty and lushness of his mountain surroundings, but he can also see the waste from an abandoned coal mine slowly sliding toward the family land. Faced with a potential avalanche of coal waste, M.C. initially wants his family to leave the mountain, but his father refuses to abandon the burial ground of his ancestors. By the end of the novel, M.C. comes to realize that, like his father, he has his own deep connection to the mountain. A young reader's novel that teens and adults will also enjoy, *M.C. Higgins, the Great* delves into the unexpected relationships a young man can have with strangers and with his home.

Grade 4 to Adult

The People Could Fly: American Black Folktales

(1985)

Virginia Hamilton. Illustrations by Leo and Diane Dillon

178 pages

Funny, gripping tales of trickster foxes, naughty children, and "stuck up" lions fill the pages of this book. A collection of twenty-four African American folktales for children, *The People Could Fly* aims to do more than entertain. Acclaimed writer and folklorist Virginia Hamilton introduces children to the history behind the folklore, a story that's just as interesting as the tales themselves. In her introduction to the book, Hamilton notes that all the stories exist because of the oppression of Africans in American slavery. For the slaves who told them, these tales were an inventive way to make sense of a horrible new environment; equally important to Hamilton is the love and hope to be found in them. The delightful black-and-white illustrations add to the spark of the stories. *The People Could Fly* is a rich celebration of African American folklore that will entertain and educate, perfect for reading aloud.

Grade 4 to Adult

Black Folktales

(1969)

Julius Lester. Illustrations by Tom Feelings

159 pages

Have you ever wondered why snakes have rattles, why people can't touch the sky, or who came up with the word *butterfly?* The answers to these questions and more can be found in this wonderful collection of folktales skillfully retold by Julius Lester. The stories in this book were not intended to be written down, but rather to be spoken aloud. In the oral tradition, storytellers add their own personal touch to the story, creating slightly different versions. The stories in *Black Folktales* have been passed along for hundreds of years. Julius Lester carries on the storyteller tradition by putting his own stamp on them, throwing in bits of 1960s pop culture and humor—in one story, the Lord is busy planning a vacation and reading *TV Guide*. This riveting collection of classic African American folklore will entertain and amuse and teach readers a thing or two as well.

Grade 4 to Adult

The Dark-Thirty: Southern Tales of the Supernatural
(1992)
Patricia C. McKissack. Illustrations by Brian Pinkney
122 pages

In this collection of mysterious folktales, the American South becomes the setting for encounters between the everyday and the supernatural. In one story, a Ku Klux Klan member is haunted by the ghost of the man who was lynched after the Klan member framed him for murder. In another, a retired Pullman porter urgently works to delay the arrival of his own death on the famed 11:59 train. In these stories, the good are rewarded and the evil are often punished by forces beyond the grave. Many of the stories come from acclaimed author Patricia McKissack's own childhood, when her grandmother would spin bone-chilling tales during the last half hour of daylight—which the children called "the dark-thirty." Brian Pinkney's eerie black-and-white illustrations suit the mood of these tales perfectly, adding to their intrigue. Look through this collection for a dramatic introduction to the supernatural side of African American folklore.

Grade 4 to Adult

A Hero Ain't Nothin' but a Sandwich

(1973)
Alice Childress
126 pages

Now I am thirteen, but when I was a chile, it was hard to be a chile because my block is a tough block...." So begins this novel, written in a range of voices, from the captivating, often disturbing street talk of this teenager, to the voice of the tired, discouraged school principal waiting for retirement. In this classic story about drug abuse, Alice Childress introduces readers to Benjie Johnson, age thirteen, sharp and capable but also a habitual heroin user. Benjie speaks for many drug users who are confident that they are in control of their habits. As the point of view shifts from Benjie to his friend Jimmy-Lee, to his family, teachers at school, and others, readers encounter more of the politics of teenage drug use. This book has stood the test of time as an unusually sympathetic treatment of a tragic issue.

Grade 7 to Adult

The Best of Simple
(1961)

Langston Hughes. Illustrations by Bernhard Nast

245 pages

J esse B. Semple, known as Simple, is always ready to offer his opinion, whether about women, foot pain, art and culture, segregation, or taxes. At his neighborhood bar in Harlem, Simple discusses his day-to-day activities and thoughts with his bartender friend, who always offers practical advice that Simple never follows. Their conversations are very funny—Simple's seemingly "simple" observations about life always have the ring of truth to them, and are sure to make a person laugh. Yet, at the same time, issues of race and inequality figure in many of the stories and the reader can feel Simple's pain and anger lingering beneath the surface humor. Each story is quite short—just a few pages long—and the many stories filling this book can be enjoyed individually or as a whole. *The Best of Simple* is a testimony to the diverse talent of Langston Hughes, who has also achieved great success writing poetry, drama, and longer fiction.

Grade 7 to Adult

Hoops: A Novel

(1981)
Walter Dean Myers
183 pages

L onnie Jackson has grown up with a basketball in hand. He has always used basketball to escape from his problems—as Lonnie puts it, "My game was my fame, and I knew it was together." When a citywide basketball tournament is organized, Lonnie's coach, Cal, turns out to be a huge influence on him. At first Lonnie resists Cal, but the man eventually earns his respect with his skills and knowledge of basketball. Lonnie and Cal develop a special relationship that will get Lonnie through some difficult times. Cal played professionally once, but threw everything away by getting involved in a gambling ring. The coach's experience teaches Lonnie that however great his basketball game is, he must have an equally good game plan for the rest of his life. Told from the often humorous and biting point of view of a teenager living in Harlem, this novel is an important exploration of the opportunities and pitfalls in the dream of basketball stardom.

Grade 7 to Adult

The ball felt good in my hands. When I went up for a shot from the top of the key, it was as if I had never let the ball go, like I was reaching from the top of the key and directing the ball into the hoop.

Walter Dean Myers
Hoops: A Novel

Somewhere in the Darkness

(1992)

Walter Dean Myers

168 pages

W alter Dean Myers explores the growing relationship between a father and son who barely know each other in this serious novel for young people. Fifteen-year-old Jimmy Little has grown up with the knowledge that his absent father is in jail for killing a man during a robbery. Jimmy has had no contact with him since he was a small child. Jimmy's mom is dead, but one of her best friends, known to Jimmy as Mama Jean, raises him as if he were her own.

All of the comfort and stability in Jimmy's life disappears when his father, who goes by the name of Crab, shows up one day to claim his son. Jimmy and Crab travel around the country, in the process making awkward but genuine attempts to get to know each other. Serious and contemplative, this novel will keep teenagers glued to the page with anticipation as they wait—much as Jimmy does— to see if Crab is serious about being a father, or if he will disappoint again.

Grade 7 to Adult

The Learning Tree

(1963)

Gordon Parks

303 pages

W hen *The Learning Tree* opens, a dangerous cyclone is brewing, but twelve-year-old Newt Winger is too busy studying an anthill to take cover. It's up to nineteen-year-old Big Mabel to lead the boy to shelter. The story of Newt's rapid transformation from childhood to adolescence begins with the loss of his virginity to Big Mabel during the storm and continues through the death of his mother and the breakup of his family as he is sent "up North" to live with an aunt. In this intensely personal book written with gentle compassion, Gordon Parks dramatizes Newt's adolescent encounters with sex, first love, approaching manhood, and the death of loved ones. Though this is the first work of fiction by the multitalented photographer, journalist, poet, filmmaker, and composer, *The Learning Tree* reflects Parks's continuing celebration of African American family life and strength.

Grade 7 to Adult

The Well: David's Story

(1995)

Mildred D. Taylor

92 pages

This captivating story takes readers back to a summer in the early 1900s, when the Logans are the only family in their area whose well hasn't gone dry. The Logans show their characteristic generosity and fairness by sharing their well water with everyone who needs it, regardless of whether they are black, white, nasty, or kind. David, one of the Logan children, learns that his family's generosity means nothing to their white neighbors, the Simms family, whose teenage sons think that their whiteness gives them the right to be vicious tyrants. David's thirteen-year-old brother, Hammer, refuses to accept demeaning, abusive treatment from anyone—especially from those who depend on his own family's generosity for the water they need to live. He stands up for himself and David, getting the boys in a heap of trouble. In the end, the Simms boys get what they deserve, but only at the expense of the whole community. Written in the warm, engaging style of someone telling a story out loud, *The Well* is a moving portrayal of the tragedy of racism.

Grade 7 to Adult

Charlie Simms was always mean, and that's the truth of it. Thing is we never knew just how mean he was until that year back when all the wells in our part of Mississippi went dry. All the wells except ours, that is.

Mildred Taylor
The Well: David's Story

Rite of Passage

(1994)

Richard Wright. Afterword by Arnold Rampersad

151 pages

J ohnny Gibbs leads the happy, normal life of a loved, bright fifteen-year-old until he comes home from school one day to find his mother crying and his suitcase sitting in the hallway. As the story unfolds, Johnny finds out that he is not the biological son of the parents who have raised him since he was a baby, but a foster child. Now, against everyone's wishes, "the City folks" have decided to move Johnny to a new foster home. Suddenly faced with so much upheaval, Johnny takes control of his life the only way he knows how: he runs away. Johnny becomes involved in a teenage gang, but his new life on the streets gives him no comfort. The teenage boys in this novel come across as innocent children in a tainted, often violent and profane world, showing that even teenagers still need the stability and comfort of a family. Published for the first time more than thirty years after Richard Wright's death, *Rite of Passage* is a moving introduction to the brilliant, often brutal fiction of this renowned writer.

Grade 7 to Adult

Go Tell It on the Mountain

(1953)

James Baldwin

303 pages

Drawing on James Baldwin's own experiences growing up, *Go Tell It on the Mountain* paints a picture of childhood faith giving way to doubt and painful self-exploration. The story revolves around John Grimes, whom everyone has always expected to follow in his father's footsteps and become a preacher. For the Grimes family, the black church and its spirituals represent power and tradition. Baldwin's forceful, poetic writing invites readers to share John's terror when he realizes that he has serious doubts about his religious faith. As a young man just discovering his sexuality, John sees contradictions between the flesh and the spirit. Problems with his difficult, demanding, and often hypocritical father further complicate his outlook. Portraying the conflict between artistic sensuality and religious righteousness, this intense novel is a powerful introduction to a recurring theme in Baldwin's writing.

Grade 10 to Adult

If Beale Street Could Talk

(1974)

James Baldwin

197 pages

J ames Baldwin casts a somber shadow in this hauntingly beautiful novel about a young couple in love whose dreams are nearly crushed by the burdens of racism and poverty. Fonny and Tish are planning to get married and live in a loft in New York City, where Fonny can sculpt. Then, a policeman known to be racist and abusive arrests Fonny for a crime he did not commit: rape. While Fonny awaits trial in a jail cell, Tish learns that she is going to have his baby. Even though it is obvious the evidence against Fonny is shaky and smacks of a set-up, getting him out of jail seems almost impossible. But Tish's family fights for his freedom, working desperately to get Fonny out before prison leaves its ugly mark on him forever, as it has on so many other men in their neighborhood. *If Beale Street Could Talk* is more than a simple love story—it is also a sobering look at a justice system that mocks truth and freedom. With this story, its passion and vivid love scenes, James Baldwin has crafted a novel so compelling that it will linger in readers' minds for a long time to come.

Grade 10 to Adult

And I remember that at that moment everything stood still. The sun didn't move and the earth didn't move, the sky stared down, waiting, and I put my hand on my heart to make it start beating again.

James Baldwin
If Beale Street Could Talk

Brotherman: The Odyssey of Black Men in America

(1995)

Edited by Herb Boyd and Robert L. Allen. Illustrations
by Tom Feelings

909 pages

Brotherman is a comprehensive collection of fiction,
poetry, and nonfiction from black male writers, past and
present. Included is the work of such well-known writers as
Sterling Brown, Paul Lawrence Dunbar, and John Oliver
Killens, along with other accomplished men like Kareem
Abdul-Jabbar, Spike Lee, and Duke Ellington.

The great diversity of experience and ideology among
black men is sometimes overlooked in general discussions
of African American culture and history, but this anthology
brings it all home. Selections are organized around
themes: the masks black men wear in order to succeed;
musical innovators from bebop to hip-hop; the stories
passed down from father to son in black families; and the
importance of love in the lives of black men. *Brotherman* is
a broad and informative look at the accomplishments and
dilemmas of African American men.

Grade 10 to Adult

Platitudes

(1988)
Trey Ellis
183 pages; illustrations

Witty and adventurous, *Platitudes* is a complex novel focusing on the often wide gap between the outlooks of black men and women, present and past. Trey Ellis gives us two black authors, a man and a woman, who carry on a conversation through their writing. Dewayne Wellington is a sexist experimental novelist; Isshee Ayam is a feminist writer who criticizes excessive machismo in the writing of black men. Wellington writes a romantic story named "Platitudes." Its main characters, Earle and Dorothy, are star students at exclusive New York City schools. Ayam writes her own version of Wellington's story, taking these same characters to rural Georgia. Both of these stories appear in this book, creating an interesting story-within-the-story. This thought-provoking novel, while fun to read, will challenge readers to examine their own assumptions about gender relations.

Grade 10 to Adult

Invisible Man

(1952)
Ralph Ellison
581 pages

T his novel has often been compared to a jazz solo, in
which a musician starts out with a particular riff, improvises
a complex middle section, and ends up returning to his
first notes. *Invisible Man* works in just this kind of musical
fashion, as Ellison explores what it means to be both black
and American—to exist, but not to be seen. When the
novel opens, readers are presented with a man who says he
is invisible. Talking directly to the reader, he says he lives
underground, undetected, in a long-forgotten section of a
basement; he leads a life of exile, siphoning off electricity
to keep his 1,369 light bulbs burning. The bulk of the
novel explores the twenty-year span of events leading up
to his unusual living situation, and finally, to his self-
awareness. *Invisible Man* portrays a complicated web of hazy
confusion as a young man tries to navigate his way through
a world he does not understand. This intriguing coming-of-
age story has been hailed as a masterpiece of modern
fiction; it will keep committed readers glued to the page.

Grade 10 to Adult

Perhaps you'll think it strange that an invisible man should need light, desire light, love light. But maybe it is exactly because I am invisible. Light confirms my reality, gives birth to my form.

Ralph Ellison
Invisible Man

The Conjure-Man Dies: A Mystery Tale of Dark Harlem

(1932)
Rudolph Fisher
316 pages

T his first-rate mystery, full of intrigue and surprise, presents an intimate view of the 1930s Harlem underworld. As the story opens, the body of N'Gana Frimbo has been discovered and it is up to Detective Perry Dart and his friend, Dr. John Archer, to conduct the official investigation into his death. An unusual character for a mystery, Frimbo is recognizable from African American folklore as an African king turned American conjure-man and fortune-teller. Frimbo also happens to have been educated in philosophy at Harvard University. Magic adds an extra layer of suspense to the mystery surrounding this man's death. In this world, where nothing is what it seems, discovering who killed the conjure-man is no easy task.

Grade 10 to Adult

In My Father's House
(1978)
Ernest J. Gaines
214 pages

In *My Father's House* is set in the late 1960s. As the novel opens, a stranger has come to the small town of St. Adrienne, Louisiana. The ragged, eccentric young man calls himself Robert X, but discloses little else about himself. He is cloaked in mystery, leaving the residents both suspicious and curious. One thing becomes clear: the stranger is seeking out the town's vibrant, charismatic civil rights leader and Baptist minister, the Reverend Phillip Martin. This mysterious tale unfolds slowly, as Gaines draws out the suspense, leading readers into the true relationship between Robert X and the reverend. Robert is a reminder of a troubled past that Phillip thought he had escaped. At age sixty, the leader—sometimes compared to Martin Luther King, Jr.—is idolized in his community. Being a public figure makes it even more difficult for Phillip to confess his past troubles. With *In My Father's House*, Gaines brilliantly captures one man's personal struggles.

Grade 10 to Adult

Black Gangster

(1977)

Donald Goines

280 pages

xplicit, violent, and disturbing, *Black Gangster* is an action-packed tale of crime in the Detroit underworld. After spending four years in prison, twenty-two-year-old Prince is now determined to make a career out of crime. Tall, slim, smart, and smooth, Prince has decided to run an organization involved in bootlegging, drugs, prostitution, and other crimes. Prince's "job" is not easy, given the perseverance of police and competition from other crafty criminals. Prince's style—sometimes soft, sometimes hard—reveals the reality of the fast life on the streets. This raucous "pulp fiction" from best-selling author Donald Goines is sure to keep mature readers spellbound.

Grade 10 to Adult

Right by My Side
(1993)
David Haynes
179 pages

This brilliant novel flawlessly weaves comedy through a serious story that will be familiar to many young men. Fifteen-year-old Marshall Field Finney's eccentric mother named him after a department store. His mother decides to leave the family in their "crackerbox" in St. Louis, and go off in search of a new life. Marshall is left to fend for himself, with a father who reacts at first to his wife's abandonment not by becoming a better parent, but with his own flight into self-indulgence.

Marshall's keen eye, if not his behavior, makes him the adult in relationships not just with his father, but with his best friends as well: Todd, a white kid from the wrong side of the tracks, and Artie, the best-dressed kid in school. His insightful observations about everyone and everything are hilarious and biting. Marshall continually questions the motivations and values of the people in his own home, at his mostly white school, and in Todd's abusive family. *Right by My Side* is a novel to be savored.

Grade 10 to Adult

A Rage in Harlem

(first published as *For Love of Imabelle* in 1957)

Chester Himes

192 pages

J ackson doesn't have what it takes to be a hustler—he trusts just about everyone he meets and believes everything he hears, whether it's his sly, devious, cheating girlfriend, Imabelle, singing the merits of another risky scam, or a man who says he can turn ten-dollar bills into one-hundred-dollar bills. Jackson's naivete gets him into all sorts of trouble with the police, since he's always the one left to take the blame after pulling a fast one. His twin brother Goldy is a slick hustler who spends his days dressed up as Sister Gabriel, a "Sister of Mercy" who sells admission tickets to heaven for one dollar apiece. While this novel is sprinkled with humor, it is also very violent and sometimes cutting. The first in Himes's series of crime novels, this action-packed story about Harlem's most innocent con man will appeal to older readers.

Grade 10 to Adult

The Autobiography of an Ex-Colored Man
(1912)
James Weldon Johnson
211 pages

This extraordinary novel was originally published anonymously in 1912 and was widely assumed to be a genuine autobiography, although the main character is fictional. The nameless narrator grapples with the dilemma of passing for white or acknowledging his black identity. He movingly conveys the complexity of this difficult decision, seeing clearly the practical advantages of being white, while cherishing the rich cultural history of African Americans. His mother, who is black, has raised him with a sense of pride in his black identity, and this carries him through many difficult moments. Yet the identity question troubles him most of his life, and his eventual decision is a tortured one. The main character's experiences in New York City and travels through the American South and Europe provide insight into the realities of life for black people early in this century. When it was first published, this novel created a sensation because of its realism, and it remains a unique look at questions of racial identity.

Grade 10 to Adult

Home to Harlem

(1928)

Claude McKay

340 pages

T his novel brings to life the rich, sensuous joys of
1920s Harlem. The book's main character, Jake Brown, has
returned from fighting in World War I only to struggle
with discrimination in his own country. Jake and his friends
are young, working-class, single men in search of pleasure
and fulfillment. The novel also includes characters like
Ray, an ambitious young man from Haiti who studies
literature and dreams of improving society by teaching
others about the ideas he encounters. Easy to read, *Home to
Harlem* is a wonderful novel from acclaimed best-selling
Harlem Renaissance author, Claude McKay.

Grade 10 to Adult

Song of Solomon
(1977)
Toni Morrison
337 pages

Toni Morrison deftly captures the subtleties of a young man's quest for self-knowledge in this complex, deeply layered book. *Song of Solomon* tells the life story of Milkman Dead. Growing up in a peculiar family shrouded in secrecy about themselves and their pasts, Milkman is frustrated because he knows very little about his family's extended history, including how exactly they came to have the last name "Dead." The novel traces Milkman's quest to find out about his family, and little by little, he begins to put together the often painful pieces of their past. His search for identity is gripping and intense, and also rich in symbolism that creates a magical mood in the book. Morrison won the Pulitzer Prize for *Song of Solomon*, and it remains one of her most popular and challenging works today.

Grade 10 to Adult

Devil in a Blue Dress

(1990)
Walter Mosley
215 pages

Walter Mosley's first novel takes readers on a tour of underground Los Angeles in 1948, led by the charming and shrewd Easy Rawlins. He is in a bind as the novel opens—his mortgage payment will be due in six days, and he has just been fired from his job. When a mysterious white gangster wants to hire Easy to find a beautiful white woman who hangs out in jazz clubs, he smells trouble. However, Easy's need for quick cash overrules his common sense, and he accepts the assignment. The search for the beautiful and elusive Daphne Monet leads Easy from one gangster to another—a dangerous and exciting journey. The first in an extraordinary series of novels, this complex and layered mystery will thrill readers with its style, its vivid descriptions of Los Angeles in the late 1940s, and Easy's sharp, insightful observations on human nature.

Grade 10 to Adult

Gone Fishin'

(1997)
Walter Mosley
244 pages

Emotional and thought-provoking, this novel portrays a brief but bizarre road trip in 1939 Texas. Nineteen-year-old Easy Rawlins is accompanying his friend, Mouse, on a dubious trip from Houston to Pariah, Texas. Mouse plans to seek money—which he believes is rightfully his—from his widowed stepfather. It's not clear just how the impulsive young man intends to acquire the money—but it is clear at the outset that the trip could turn tragic or comic in an instant. During the journey, Easy experiences voodoo, violence, illness, and revelations that will change his life—including the realization that he must learn to read. For those who are familiar with Walter Mosley's writing, *Gone Fishin'* is all the more fascinating because the youthful main character is the same Easy Rawlins who appears in Mosley's acclaimed mysteries. But every reader will be riveted by this story of a thoughtful young man making the passage to adulthood.

Grade 10 to Adult

Losing Absalom

(1994)

Alexs D. Pate

305 pages

*L*osing *Absalom*, Alexs Pate's first novel, masterfully captures the subtle interactions of a family in a time of turmoil. As the novel opens, Absalom Goodman is lying in a hospital bed, with little hope that he will survive. What follows is an examination of his life—by Absalom himself and by his family. Although Absalom is so sick he can no longer speak, his voice permeates this tender novel, showing that in many families the most poignant communication is what remains unsaid. Like so many African American men, Absalom worked exceedingly long hours to support his family. He struggled to raise his son and daughter in a North Philadelphia neighborhood that slowly succumbed to the violence, drugs, and gangs that ultimately also enveloped his own household. *Losing Absalom* is an intimate, heavily layered novel that celebrates the courage and love that got men like Absalom Goodman through each day.

Grade 10 to Adult

Absalom fought what he had become. If he couldn't go forward into consciousness then he would let go and wing into the creases of clouded sky.

Alexs D. Pate
Losing Absalom

The Third Life of Grange Copeland

(1970)

Alice Walker

247 pages

T*he Third Life of Grange Copeland* takes readers from sharecropping in the 1920s up to the early civil rights movement. Grange Copeland sacrifices much of his youth working long hours for a white landowner, only to slip further and further into debt and poverty. Alice Walker brilliantly captures Grange's slow decline from a man full of love and hope to a person ready to explode with anger due to the racism and injustice he faces daily.

It is only after watching his grown son commit familiar acts of vengeance and violence upon his own innocent family that Grange fully realizes the misdirection, cruelty, and absurdity of his own life. For Grange, the healing process begins with his granddaughter, Ruth; he raises the young girl with all of the love and dignity he could not give his own son so many years before. *The Third Life of Grange Copeland* is an emotional, explicit, and compassionate look at the beauty that can reside in the midst of a family's painful journey from crisis to healing.

Grade 10 to Adult

Memory of Kin: Stories about Family by Black Writers
(1991)
Edited by Mary Helen Washington
416 pages

M *emory of Kin* is a collection of short stories about mothers, fathers, aunts, cousins, grandparents, and extended families. Many of the best-known African American authors are included—from 19th-century writer Charles Chesnutt to James Baldwin, Ernest J. Gaines, Rita Dove, Jamaica Kincaid, and others. The stories are arranged in chapters, each representing a different aspect of the family—"Mothers and Daughters," "Husbands and Wives," "Grandparents," and so on—each beginning with poetry about the subject. After many of the stories, Washington has included commentary for readers who want more information about the authors. *Memory of Kin* is a powerful tribute to the black family.

Grade 10 to Adult

The Man Who Cried I Am
(1967)
John A. Williams
403 pages

his rich novel portrays the lives of an elite group of African American artists who moved to Europe in the middle decades of this century. They left to escape the creative suffocation they experienced in the United States, only to find racism accompanying them on their journeys. As the novel opens, writer Max Reddick is sitting at his favorite café in Amsterdam, hoping to spot his ex-wife on her way home from work. He has just come from Paris, where he'd attended the funeral of his friend Henry Ames, a character modeled on author Richard Wright. Moving backward and forward in time and place, between New York and Europe, this novel follows the dizzying spiral of a writer's life buffeted by politics, racism, romance, and, finally, international conspiracy. *The Man Who Cried I Am* reads variously like a historical novel, a biography, and an action thriller. All add up to a beautifully descriptive and riveting story unlike any other.

Grade 10 to Adult

Native Son

(1940)
Richard Wright
308 pages

his electrifying—and at times explicitly sexual and violent—novel by Richard Wright introduces readers to Bigger Thomas, a young man bursting with hot, fierce emotions. Bigger cannot shut his eyes to the injustice he endures daily, nor will he blindly accept the position he has been granted by the racist society of 1940s America. Other people in Bigger's life have ways to try to cope with racism: Bigger's mother relies on religion to get through each day, while his girlfriend Bessie hides behind whiskey. Bigger cannot find solace anywhere and thus, Wright shows, he is bound for trouble. *Native Son* portrays a complicated and suspenseful chain of murder and mystery. It asks how responsible a man can be for his actions if society does not allow him to be free. The first best-selling novel by an African American author, *Native Son* continues to shock and provoke thought in readers today, more than fifty years after its original publication.

Grade 10 to Adult

History

Jambo Means Hello: Swahili Alphabet Book

(1974)

Muriel Feelings. Illustrations by Tom Feelings

Unpaged

J *ambo Means Hello* is a Swahili alphabet book designed to introduce children to one of the most widely spoken languages of Africa. The book features a Swahili word for each of the twenty-four letters of the Swahili alphabet. Feelings picks words that children will be familiar with, like "rafiki," which means friend, and "heshima," which means respect, and shows how these concepts operate in African cultures, revealing most often a strong sense of community and caring for each other. Richly textured black-and-white illustrations form a beautiful background for this fun and informative book.

Picture Book to Grade 3

The Great Migration: An American Story

(1993)

Written and illustrated by Jacob Lawrence. Poem by
Walter Dean Myers

Unpaged

B eautiful full-color paintings by Jacob Lawrence
illustrate this clear and simple history of the Great
Migration, the mass exodus of African Americans from the
rural South to the industrial North in the early part of the
twentieth century. Lawrence was born in the midst of the
Great Migration, and his personal connection to this topic
comes across in the sixty bold, colorful paintings that form
the bulk of this book. These paintings, called the
"Migration of the Negro," helped to make Lawrence
one of the most popular and respected painters of the
twentieth century. In his introduction to this book,
Lawrence describes how he tried not only to show the
hardship and sacrifice involved with migration, but also
"a kind of power, and even beauty" that can be associated
with it. Its words and pictures shining with dignity and
pride, *The Great Migration* is a book all ages can enjoy.

Picture Book, Grades 4 to 9

Extraordinary Black Americans from Colonial to Contemporary Times

(1989)
Susan Altman
240 pages; illustrations

I n *Extraordinary Black Americans,* Susan Altman fits hundreds of years of African American excellence into one intriguing, easy-to-read book. This book features short descriptions of African Americans who have made important contributions to American history. Featured are eighty-five writers, artists, athletes, activists, heroes, and other important figures. Also included are brief descriptions of important landmarks, such as Reconstruction and the Underground Railroad. Some of the book's figures, like Frederick Douglass, are already well known, while others, like Elizabeth Eckford, the first African American student to try to integrate an Arkansas high school, deserve to be. Wherever possible, Altman has paired illustrations and quotes with her writing. This is a fascinating book.

Grade 4 to Adult

Tommy Traveler in the World of Black History

(1991)

Written and illustrated by Tom Feelings

45 pages

Acclaimed illustrator Tom Feelings has combined the comic-strip style, color, and format with an unlikely subject—black history—to create this unique and engaging book. Tommy Traveler is a young boy who has read all the black history available in his library. Introduced by the librarian to a doctor who owns a huge private collection of black history books, Tommy takes off, letting his imagination carry him to key moments in African American history, and meeting up with such familiar figures as Emmett Till, Frederick Douglass, and Crispus Attucks. History comes alive here, for readers of all ages.

Grade 4 to Adult

The Black Book

(1974)

Compiled by Middleton A. Harris. Introduction by
Bill Cosby

198 pages; illustrations

he Black Book is an amazing portrait of black history.
In his introduction, Bill Cosby describes it as the imaginary
scrapbook of a "three-hundred-year-old black man." The
description fits; this book contains page after page of
miscellaneous artifacts—some well known, others
extremely personal. *The Black Book* features jokes, newspaper clippings, photographs, patents, handbills, quotes,
charms, advertisements, songs—you name it and it appears
in this book. *The Black Book* fills readers in on little-known
pockets of black history dating from the days of slavery up
to the twentieth century, and does so in an unusually
personal and direct manner. The result is a powerful book
that is spectacular both in design and content.

Grade 4 to Adult

Long Journey Home: Stories from Black History

(1972)
Julius Lester
107 pages

R enowned folklorist and historian Julius Lester believes there is more to history than the familiar stories of famous people. The stories of ordinary people are more interesting to Lester, who first researched the lives of African Americans in the nineteenth century, and then wrote short stories based on the historical facts he uncovered. Lester offers readers the Rambler, a blues guitarist who never stops moving because he doesn't want to belong to the white man. Rambling is the only way he can be free. Readers will also find intriguing the story of Louis, a slave who relied on his wits and the help of the Underground Railroad to escape—more than once. An unforgettable book, *Long Journey Home* brings to life its characters' intense will and desire for freedom.

Grade 4 to Adult

To Be a Slave

(1968)

Julius Lester. Illustrations by Tom Feelings

160 pages

J ulius Lester uses the words of ex-slaves to re-create the stories found in this powerful book. Lester draws from the accounts of white abolitionists, as well as from writers who interviewed aged ex-slaves in the 1930s and wrote down exactly what they heard. All of these accounts are vivid and personal. Many do not conform to commonly held assumptions about slavery. Julius Lester's commentary links the accounts, pointing out both unusual and common features of the experiences described. Tom Feelings's mysterious illustrations give life to the drama of the words. *To Be a Slave* is a tribute to the men and women who endured slavery.

Grade 4 to Adult

Black Diamond: The Story of the Negro Baseball Leagues

(1994)

Patricia C. McKissack and Frederick McKissack, Jr.

184 pages; illustrations

*B**lack Diamond* explores the early days of American baseball, when the color of an athlete's skin influenced his career more than his talent and skill. Even though men like "Cool Papa" Bell and Josh Gibson were some of the best baseball players around, neither man ever played integrated professional baseball in America. Instead, African Americans formed their own baseball leagues, commonly called the Negro Leagues. They also played professional baseball in Cuba and Mexico, where they were better treated and paid. *Black Diamond* covers the dawning days of the Negro Leagues and takes the story of African American baseball all the way up to the long-awaited desegregation of the major leagues in 1947, when it became possible for crossover players like Jackie Robinson, Satchel Paige, and Hank Aaron to bring their talent to a wider audience. *Black Diamond* pays tribute to these talented pioneers of baseball—men who could not be stopped.

Grade 4 to Adult

Many Thousand Gone: African Americans from Slavery to Freedom

(1993)

Virginia Hamilton. Illustrations by Leo and Diane Dillon
152 pages

In this fascinating book about slavery and the long journey to freedom, Virginia Hamilton features the stories of individuals—some famous, others known only by their first names. Each brief account is gripping, with the feel of fiction, although the events described are completely true. To escape, slaves had to think up risky, ingenious, and daring plans: Henry Brown shipped himself north in a crate, Jackson posed as his light-skinned wife's female servant on a trip to the North, and Eliza used chunks of ice as stepping stones to cross a river. The illustrations by husband-and-wife team Leo and Diane Dillon highlight the dignity and sorrow of those who directly experienced the brutalities of slavery. Like Hamilton's other books, *Many Thousand Gone* will capture the attention, imagination, and heart of anyone who glimpses within it.

Grade 7 to Adult

With the ratification of the Thirteenth Amendment to the Constitution on December 18, 1865, there was freedom, finally, for all of the 4 million African Americans.

Virginia Hamilton
Many Thousand Gone:
African Americans from
Slavery to Freedom

Red-Tail Angels: The Story of the Tuskegee Airmen of World War II

(1995)
Patricia C. and Frederick McKissack
136 pages; illustrations

In this book, husband-and-wife team Patricia and Frederick McKissack uncover the neglected story of African American pilots. Although their focus is on the United States Air Force, where African Americans were not allowed to serve until the end of World War II, this book will give readers a good sense of the events leading up to the integration. *Red-Tail Angels* takes readers back to the earliest days of aviation, introducing the first African American men and women whose love of flying spurred them to break down barriers in an aviation world that shunned women and minorities. When African Americans were finally allowed to serve in the U.S. Air Force, they initially met discrimination, harassment, and broken promises from the government, yet even this blatant mistreatment could not stop these courageous pilots. *Red-Tail Angels* is a thoughtful and proud tribute to these heroes.

Grade 7 to Adult

Now Is Your Time! The African-American Struggle for Freedom

(1991)

Walter Dean Myers

292 pages; illustrations

Walter Dean Myers approaches African American history with energy, reverence, and pride in *Now Is Your Time! The African-American Struggle for Freedom*. Myers uses his incredible skills as a storyteller to describe the lives of individuals like abolitionist James Forten and writer Ida B. Wells. He also explains the impact of such events as the Civil War and the Supreme Court decision in *Plessy* vs. *Ferguson* on the lives of African Americans in general. Walter Dean Myers's skills as a writer of fiction and poetry make this book of history lively and captivating.

Grade 7 to Adult

Blues People: Negro Music in White America

(1963)

Imamu Amiri Baraka (formerly LeRoi Jones)

244 pages

*B*lues People is an intellectual exploration of the connection between history and music in African American culture written with pride, wit, and intelligence. Amiri Baraka, born LeRoi Jones, examines the social and historical roots of spirituals, blues, jazz, swing, and rock and roll. Music, says Baraka, has always been an expression of individuality for black people in white-controlled America. Because slavery, segregation, and discrimination closed off many means of personal expression for African Americans, passionate and challenging music arose from what Baraka calls a "blues impulse." The author's skills as a cultural historian add power to this memorable tracing of black musical traditions from the time of slavery to the early phases of the rock era. With this book, Baraka has created a convincing case for his theory of the relationship between racial segregation and musical innovation. For the very serious student of black history and music, this book is a work of fascinating literature.

Grade 10 to Adult

The Middle Passage:
White Ships/Black Cargo
(1995)

Tom Feelings. Introduction by John Henrik Clarke

Unpaged

At the opening of this book, Tom Feelings offers a moving and revealing explanation of why he created *The Middle Passage*, yet there is no way to prepare for the astonishing illustrations that follow. The Middle Passage refers to the journey of slave ships from West Africa to North and South America and the Caribbean. As many as thirty to sixty million Africans were subjected to this inhumane and unimaginable crime. Feelings's black-and-white illustrations convey the anguish of this journey, starting with the capture of the African prisoners, and continuing through image after image of the long journey itself. These pictures are at once horrifying and bewitching, yet it is precisely the mysterious beauty of the illustrations which—despite the horrific subject matter—conveys the enduring strength of the African spirit. *The Middle Passage* is a magnificent achievement that adults should page through hand-in-hand with young people.

Grade 10 to Adult

Poetry

Everett Anderson's Goodbye

(1983)

Lucille Clifton. Illustrations by Ann Grifalconi

Unpaged

Lucille Clifton portrays a young boy grieving after the death of his father in this intensely emotional picture book. *Everett Anderson's Goodbye* is a poem based on the five stages of grief: denial, anger, bargaining, depression, and acceptance. Clifton actually shows Everett experiencing these stages. On one page, he's so angry that he tells his mother he does not love her. On another, he pleads with her, saying, "I will do everything you say if Daddy can be alive today." The black-and-white illustrations by Ann Grifalconi portray the full range of Everett's pain. Eventually, Everett finds a way to accept his dad's death, as he realizes that after someone dies, "love doesn't stop, and neither will I." Readers of all ages who have experienced a similar loss will identify with the young boy. This is a magnificent book to read and discuss with a young child.

Picture Book

Nathaniel Talking

(1988)

Eloise Greenfield. Illustrations by Jan Spivey Gilchrist

Unpaged

N*athaniel Talking* is a collection of poems written from the point of view of nine-year-old Nathaniel B. Free. As he says in the opening poem, "Nathaniel's Rap," he will be talking about "my philosophy / about the things I do / and the people I see." Eloise Greenfield's poems let the young boy's thoughtful personality shine. Nathaniel raps about making friends, misbehaving, missing his mother, who died the year before, and many other aspects of his life. A few of these poems, "My Daddy" and "Watching the World Go By," are written in the style of the twelve-bar blues. At the end of the book, Greenfield explains the structure of this musical form and invites young readers to write their own blues poems. The black-and-white illustrations by Jan Spivey Gilchrist reveal Nathaniel's energy and self-esteem. *Nathaniel Talking* will inspire young people to write their own poems and raps about the world.

Picture Book

How Sweet the Sound: African-American Songs for Children

(1995)

Edited by Wade and Cheryl Hudson. Illustrations by Floyd Cooper

48 pages

T his beautiful and uplifting book showcases centuries of African American music. Included are lyrics from songs like "Kum Ba Ya," which originated in Africa, as well as more contemporary hits like James Brown's "Say It Loud, I'm Black and I'm Proud." Floyd Cooper's excellent color illustrations form the backdrop for the lyrics. With spirituals, work chants, civil rights anthems, and more, *How Sweet the Sound* celebrates the important place music has had in the history of African Americans. The book also includes history about each song, as well as sheet music. This fabulous book promises to open new avenues of wonder for children and the adults who read it with them.

Picture Book to Grade 6

Pass It On: African-American Poetry for Children

(1993)

Edited by Wade Hudson. Illustrations by Floyd Cooper

32 pages

This collection of poetry flies in the face of the notion that poetry is best reserved for adults. Wade Hudson draws on the rich variety of African American poetry, offering readers poems ranging from Mari Evans's inspirational "I Can," to Eloise Greenfield's whimsical "To Catch a Fish" and Countee Cullen's serious "Incident." In his introduction, Hudson notes poetry's special place in the African American oral tradition. The poems that make up this volume are perfect choices to read aloud. Not only does this book bring together some of the best African American poetry, but Floyd Cooper's engaging color illustrations capture the feeling behind each poem and invite the reader's imagination to continue the story. As the title suggests, *Pass It On* is a collection of poetry to be shared.

Picture Book to Grade 6

Red Dog, Blue Fly: Football Poems

(1991)

Sharon Bell Mathis. Illustrations by Jan Spivey Gilchrist

Unpaged

Sharon Bell Mathis brings the excitement and energy of football to the world of poetry in this invigorating picture book. Each poem focuses on an aspect of a young boy's football season: practicing signals and plays, scoring touchdowns, dealing with injuries, and eating "playoff pizza" are just a few topics. The poem "Quarterback" pulses with the concentration needed to throw an excellent pass, while "Football" echoes the frustration of a young boy just learning to play the game. Speaking to his football, he pleads, "You sail above my fingers / you sail above my head / why not sail / into my hands instead." The poems that fill *Red Dog, Blue Fly* are best when read aloud. Jan Spivey Gilchrist's illustrations convey football's raw emotion and energy by filling the pages with vibrant color. This book will get a young boy excited about football *and* about poetry.

Picture Book, Grades 4 to 6

Sing to the Sun:
Poems and Pictures
(1992)

Written and illustrated by Ashley Bryan

Unpaged

S*ing to the Sun* is a charming introduction to poetry that adults will enjoy sharing with young children. The poems in this book are light-hearted and a joy to read, but also provide food for thought.

The opening poem, "Song," sets the tone for the rest of the book, urging readers to "sing to the sun" because "it will listen / and warm your words." Accompanying each poem is a colorful African-influenced painting made up of shapes like those in stained-glass windows. Words cannot describe the charm and beauty to be found in this lively, imaginative book.

Picture Book, Grades 4 to 9

Soul Looks Back in Wonder

(1993)

Edited and illustrated by Tom Feelings

Unpaged

Tom Feelings pairs his own artwork with the poetry of
thirteen African American authors in this thought-
provoking book for young people. He created the book to
bring forth the flow of African creativity, "searching for
new ways to connect the ancient with the new, the young
with the old, the unborn with the ancestors." These poems
are rich with pride in their African heritage and stress
strength, knowledge, brotherhood, and other virtues.
Poems by Rashidah Ismaili, Langston Hughes, Alexis De
Veaux, Margaret Walker, Lucille Clifton, and others fill
each page with energy and vitality. Feelings's illustrations
bring to life the story of each poem. With *Soul Looks Back
in Wonder*, Feelings has created a beautiful book with a
strong message.

Picture Book, Grade 7 to Adult

The Dream Keeper and Other Poems

(1932)

Langston Hughes. Illustrations by Helen Sewell

77 pages

Zeal for life, pride in his African American heritage, and the beauty of simplicity characterize this collection of poems written for young people by Langston Hughes. As spellbinding today as when they were written, these poems will draw readers into the world he created. Many of them ("I, Too," "The Negro Speaks of Rivers,") are considered masterpieces of American poetry, but all serve as examples of the beautiful, inspirational, often humorous quality of Langston Hughes's writing. The poems are organized by theme into imaginative clusters such as "Sea Charm" and "Walkers with the Dawn." *The Dream Keeper and Other Poems* is the perfect book to introduce a new generation to the poetry of Langston Hughes.

Grades 4 to 9

The Block: Poems

(1995)

Langston Hughes. Collage by Romare Bearden.
Introduction by Bill Cosby
32 pages

T *he Block* links the poetry of Langston Hughes to a
work of art by Romare Bearden, creating an explosion of
color and words. This book celebrates Harlem and reveals
the genius of both these great African American artists.
Bearden's collage, with its mixture of photos and painted
shapes, shows the people, energy, action, and emotions of
a single block in Harlem. Langston Hughes's poetry, which
is placed alongside various sections of the collage, offers a
deeper look into the feelings and personalities of the faces
in the art. Poems like "As Befits a Man" and "Madam's
Calling Cards" paint pictures of memorable personalities,
as readers meet a man who imagines a dozen pretty
women crying at his funeral, and a woman who hankers to
see her name in print. *The Block* is a stunning, lively look at
the work of two artists who are enjoyed by adults and
young people alike.

Grade 7 to Adult

For My People
(1942)
Margaret Walker. Foreword by Stephen Vincent Benet
58 pages

For My People, Margaret Walker's first collection of poetry, is an inspirational celebration of African Americans, past and present. Poems like "We Have Been Believers," "For My People," and "Since 1619" echo with voices from the past. Walker brings these voices new life, blending them with her own to create a richly textured poetry that rings with pain and pride. But as much as these poems owe to the past, they also look to a brighter future for African Americans. This book also includes some lively poems featuring key figures from African American folklore like Molly Means and Bad Man Stagolee. The straightforward style and depth of emotion and meaning to be found in For My People will charm even those who shy away from poetry.

Grade 7 to Adult

The Complete Collected Poems of Maya Angelou

(1994)

Maya Angelou

273 pages

The *Complete Collected Poems of Maya Angelou* is deep, clear, and refreshing—the perfect book to dive into for a break from the stress of everyday life. Every published volume of poetry Angelou has ever written appears here, including "On the Pulse of Morning," the poem that charmed the nation after Angelou read it at President Clinton's inauguration. Readers flipping through this collection will find lively and biting rhymed poems such as "Times-Square-Shoeshine-Composition," as well as longer, more contemplative poems like "Still I Rise." Throughout the collection two qualities remain constant: resilience and strength. This collection of Maya Angelou's poetry showcases decades of her work—each poem full of the brilliance that has become her trademark and made her one of America's most distinguished poets.

Grade 10 to Adult

Just like hopes springing high,
Still I'll rise.

Maya Angelou
"Still I Rise"
The Complete Collected Poems
of Maya Angelou

A Dark and Splendid Mass

(1992)

Mari Evans

62 pages

T he poems in *A Dark and Splendid Mass* bend and sway,
quietly grabbing a reader's attention. Mari Evans is an
acclaimed poet who first gained recognition in the 1960s;
her poems take on a distinctly contemporary tone in this
collection. Frequently, she delves into themes of love,
passion, and betrayal, as in the poem "The Catalyst," which
describes a man whose smile is so intoxicating that women
become addicted to it. Evans also writes about children: "A
Rock for Sheltering" describes the nourishment that every
child deserves. Social crimes such as poverty and racism
also appear in her poetry—Evans dedicates "Alabama
Landscape" to African Americans who have lost their lives
to police brutality. Mature readers of *A Dark and Splendid
Mass* will find consistently important messages in poems
full of strength.

Grade 10 to Adult

In Search of Color Everywhere: A Collection of African-American Poetry

(1994)

Edited by E. Ethelbert Miller. Illustrations by Terrance Cummings

256 pages

Featuring writers as diverse as Bob Kaufman, Phillis Wheatley, and Haki Madhubuti, this expressive book captures the rich variety of African American poetry spanning centuries of experience. Rather than arranging its poems by date, this book groups them by themes such as "Freedom," "Healing Poems," and "Celebration of Blackness." The result is that readers will find Margaret Walker's "For My People" sharing a page with Public Enemy's "Party for Your Right to Fight." Readers will find similar mind-opening comparisons throughout. *In Search of Color Everywhere* does more than showcase the poetry of more than one hundred talented writers; it also provides a rousing and unique glimpse into African American history.

Grade 10 to Adult

Read with the Children

Storytelling is one of the great traditions of African American culture. Today, our authors tell stories, and all of us join in the tradition when we read and talk about books with each other and with our children. And just as Tom Feelings's *Middle Passage*—a story told in pictures—is a continuation of this practice, we hope *Spirited Minds* will also take its place in upholding this great tradition.

The custom of storytelling has endured because of its force: there is no better way to teach than to engage the imagination. Anyone who has ever been captivated by a book knows the power of the imagination to expand the mind. Such vivid sensations are evoked by a good book that reading can stimulate a thirst for knowledge, foster empathy, and encourage curiosity—all traits that develop from life experiences. It is for this reason that *Spirited Minds* includes literature representing such a broad range of subjects. Just as the storytelling tradition is about many stories told again and again, one to the next, reading isn't about one book, but about a lifetime of books. Not just novels, but histories, plays, biographies, and poems all tell a story from which we gain knowledge.

This is reason enough to share books with children and young adults. But there are other reasons, critical to even the very youngest child. We know the thrill of reading a picture book like *Max Found Two Sticks* or *John Henry* with a child at our side, but doing so is more than just having fun. By giving the child a chance to become familiar with the sight of words and their meanings, we're preparing him or her to flourish in school. Further, the warmth and affection of the situation teaches the child to associate those feelings with reading: a kindness that a child will never forget, and the beginnings of a love for reading that will enrich an entire life.

Along with providing a shared experience unlike any other, reading and discussing literature with the child or young adult allows you to confront difficult questions outside the heat of the experience. This makes reading with small groups of young people especially valuable; books can give you the opportunity to talk about every imaginable topic.

For teens, who are going through so many changes, having a chance to read and talk about a character or person they can relate to, like David in *The Well* or Nathan McCall in *Makes Me Wanna Holler,* can help them make sense of complex feelings. At the same time, learning about their own cultural history in *The Black Book* or about others from a different time or place can give young people some perspective on their own lives, and foster a strong sense of identity. And for all readers, the sheer genius of masterworks like *Native Son* or *The Complete Collected Poems of Maya Angelou* can nurture a tremendous sense of pride.

When we engender a love for reading in our chidren—by bringing books into their lives, by reading to them and with them—we expand their world immeasurably.

Index of Books by Title

Alvin Ailey. Andrea Davis Pinkney. Illustrations by Brian Pinkney. New York: Hyperion Books for Children, 1993. *9*

The Amen Corner: A Play. James Baldwin. New York: Dial Press, 1968. *35*

The Autobiography of an Ex-Colored Man. James Weldon Johnson. Boston: Sherman, French and Co., 1912. *89*

The Autobiography of LeRoi Jones. Imamu Amiri Baraka. New York: Freundlich Books, 1984. *22*

The Autobiography of Malcolm X. Malcolm X and Alex Haley. Introduction by M.S. Handler. Epilogue by Alex Haley. New York: Grove Press, 1965. *24*

The Best of Simple. Langston Hughes. Illustrations by Bernhard Nast. New York: Hill and Wang, 1961. *69*

The Big Sea: An Autobiography. Langston Hughes. New York: Knopf, 1940. *16*

The Black Book. Compiled by Middleton A. Harris. Introduction by Bill Cosby. New York: Random House, 1974. *106*

Black Boy: A Record of Childhood and Youth. Richard Wright. New York and London: Harper & Brothers, 1945. *31*

Black Diamond: The Story of the Negro Baseball Leagues. Patricia C. McKissack and Frederick McKissack, Jr. New York: Scholastic, 1994. *109*

Black Folktales. Julius Lester. Illustrations by Tom Feelings. New York: Richard W. Baron Publishing Co., 1969. *66*

Black Gangster. Donald Goines. Los Angeles: Holloway House, 1977. *86*

The Block: Poems. Langston Hughes. Collage by Romare Bearden. Introduction by Bill Cosby. New York: Viking, 1995. *126*

Blues People: Negro Music in White America. Imamu Amiri Baraka. Originally published under the author's earlier name: LeRoi Jones. New York: Morrow, 1963. *114*

Brotherman: The Odyssey of Black Men in America. Edited by Herb Boyd and Robert L. Allen. Illustrations by Tom Feelings. New York: One World, 1995. *80*

Brothers and Keepers. John Edgar Wideman. New York: Holt, Rinehart and Winston, 1984. *30*

Chevrolet Saturdays. Candy Dawson Boyd. New York: Macmillan, 1993. *59*

A Choice of Weapons. Gordon Parks. New York: Harper & Row, 1966. *28*

Clean Your Room, Harvey Moon! Written and illustrated by Pat Cummings. New York: Bradbury Press, 1991. *50*

Coming Home: From the Life of Langston Hughes. Written and illustrated by Floyd Cooper. New York: Philomel Books, 1994. *8*

The Complete Collected Poems of Maya Angelou. Maya Angelou. New York: Random House, 1994. *128*

The Conjure-Man Dies: A Mystery Tale of Dark Harlem. Rudolph Fisher. First published in New York in 1932. *84*

Creative Fire. Editors of Time-Life Books. Alexandria, VA: Time-Life Books, 1994. *14*

A Dark and Splendid Mass. Mari Evans. New York: Harlem River Press, 1992. *130*

The Darker Face of the Earth: A Verse Play in Fourteen Scenes. Rita Dove. Illustrations by Mark Woolley. Brownsville, OR: Story Line Press, 1994. *42*

The Dark-Thirty: Southern Tales of the Supernatural. Patricia C. McKissack. Illustrations by Brian Pinkney. New York: Knopf, 1992. *67*

The Day the Bronx Died. Michael Henry Brown. New York: Applause, 1996. *41*

Days of Grace: A Memoir. Arthur Ashe and Arnold Rampersad. New York: Knopf, 1993. *20*

Devil in a Blue Dress. Walter Mosley. New York: Norton, 1990. *92*

The Dream Keeper and Other Poems. Langston Hughes. Illustrations by Helen Sewell. New York: Knopf, 1932. *125*

Dutchman and The Slave, Two Plays. Imamu Amiri Baraka. Originally published under the author's earlier name: LeRoi Jones. New York: Morrow, 1964. *40*

Escape to Freedom: A Play about Young Frederick Douglass. Ossie Davis. New York: Penguin, 1976. *34*

Everett Anderson's Goodbye. Lucille Clifton. Illustrations by Ann Grifalconi. New York: Holt, Rinehart and Winston, 1983. *118*

Extraordinary Black Americans from Colonial to Contemporary Times. Susan Altman. Chicago: Childrens Press, 1989. *104*

The Fire Next Time. James Baldwin. New York: Dial Press, 1963. *21*

Five Plays. Langston Hughes. Introduction by Webster Smalley. Bloomington, IN: Indiana University Press, 1963. *43*

For My People. Margaret Walker. Foreword by Stephen Vincent Benet. New Haven: Yale University Press, 1942. *127*

Four Lives in the Bebop Business. A.B. Spellman. New York: Pantheon, 1966. *29*

The Friendship. Mildred D. Taylor. Illustrations by Max Ginsburg. New York: Dial Books for Young Readers, 1987. *61*

The Gift-Giver. Joyce Hansen. New York: Houghton Mifflin/Clarion Books, 1980. *60*

Go Tell It on the Mountain. James Baldwin. New York: Knopf, 1953. *77*

The Man Who Cried I Am. John A. Williams. Boston: Little, Brown, 1967. *98*

Many Thousand Gone: African Americans from Slavery to Freedom. Virginia Hamilton. Illustrations by Leo and Diane Dillon. New York: Knopf, 1993. *110*

Marcus Garvey. Mary Lawler. Introduction by Coretta Scott King. New York: Chelsea House, 1988. *11*

Max Found Two Sticks. Written and illustrated by Brian Pinkney. New York: Simon & Schuster Books for Young Readers, 1994. *52*

M.C. Higgins, the Great. Virginia Hamilton. New York: Macmillan, 1974. *64*

Memory of Kin: Stories about Family by Black Writers. Edited by Mary Helen Washington. New York: Doubleday, 1991. *97*

The Middle Passage: White Ships/Black Cargo. Tom Feelings. Introduction by John Henrik Clarke. New York: Dial Books, 1995. *115*

Mule Bone: A Comedy of Negro Life. Langston Hughes and Zora Neale Hurston. New York: HarperPerennial, 1991. *44*

My Friend Jacob. Lucille Clifton. Illustrations by Thomas DiGrazia. New York: Dutton, 1980. *49*

Narrative of the Life of Frederick Douglass, an American Slave, Written by Himself. Frederick Douglass. Preface signed by William Lloyd Garrison. Boston: Anti-Slavery Office, 1849. *13*

Nathaniel Talking. Eloise Greenfield. Illustrations by Jan Spivey Gilchrist. New York: Black Butterfly Children's Books, 1988. *119*

The National Black Drama Anthology: Eleven Plays from America's Leading African American Theaters. Edited by Woodie King, Jr. New York: Applause, 1995. *45*

Native Son. Richard Wright. New York and London: Harper & Brothers, 1940. *99*

No Free Ride: From the Mean Streets to the Mainstream. Kweisi Mfume and Ron Stodghill II. New York: One World, 1996. *27*

Now Is Your Time! The African-American Struggle for Freedom. Walter Dean Myers. New York: HarperTrophy, 1991. *113*

Pass It On: African-American Poetry for Children. Edited by Wade Hudson. Illustrations by Floyd Cooper. New York: Scholastic, 1993. *121*

The People Could Fly: American Black Folktales. Virginia Hamilton. Illustrations by Leo and Diane Dillon. New York: Knopf, 1985. *65*

The Piano Lesson. August Wilson. New York: Dutton, 1990. *38*

Platitudes. Trey Ellis. New York: Vintage Books, 1988. *81*

A Rage in Harlem. Chester Himes. First published as *For Love of Imabelle* in 1957. *88*

A Raisin in the Sun: A Drama in Three Acts. Lorraine Hansberry. New York: Random House, 1959. *36*

Red Dog, Blue Fly: Football Poems. Sharon Bell Mathis. Illustrations by Jan Spivey Gilchrist. New York: Viking, 1991. *122*

Red-Tail Angels: The Story of the Tuskegee Airmen of World War II. Patricia C. and Frederick McKissack. New York: Walker and Co., 1995. *112*

Right by My Side. David Haynes. Minneapolis: New Rivers Press, 1993. *87*

Rite of Passage. Richard Wright. Afterword by Arnold Rampersad. New York: HarperCollins, 1994. *76*

Sidewalk Story. Sharon Bell Mathis. Illustrations by Leo Carty. New York: Viking, 1971. *58*

Sing to the Sun: Poems and Pictures. Written and illustrated by Ashley Bryan. New York: HarperCollins, 1992. *123*

Soledad Brother: The Prison Letters of George Jackson. George Jackson. Introduction by Jean Genet. New York: Coward-McCann, 1970. *23*

Somewhere in the Darkness. Walter Dean Myers. New York: Scholastic, 1992. *72*

Song of Solomon. Toni Morrison. New York: Knopf, 1977. *91*

Soul Looks Back in Wonder. Edited and illustrated by Tom Feelings. New York: Dial Books, 1993. *124*

The Stories Julian Tells. Ann Cameron. Illustrations by Ann Strugnell. New York: Pantheon Books, 1981. *56*

Storm in the Night. Mary Stolz. Illustrations by Pat Cummings. New York: Harper & Row, 1988. *54*

Sugar Ray. Sugar Ray Robinson and Dave Anderson. New York: Viking, 1970. *19*

The Sweet Flypaper of Life. Roy DeCarava and Langston Hughes. New York: Simon & Schuster, 1955. *63*

The Third Life of Grange Copeland. Alice Walker. Harcourt Brace Jovanovich, 1970. *96*

To Be a Slave. Julius Lester. Illustrations by Tom Feelings. New York: Dial Press, 1968. *108*

Tommy Traveler in the World of Black History. Written and illustrated by Tom Feelings. New York: Black Butterfly Children's Books, 1991. *105*

Twilight: Los Angeles, 1992. On the Road: A Search for American Character. Anna Deavere Smith. New York: Anchor Books, 1994. *37*

The Watsons Go to Birmingham—1963. Christopher Paul Curtis. New York: Delacorte Press, 1995. *62*

W.E.B. Du Bois: A Biography. Virginia Hamilton. New York: Crowell, 1972. *15*

The Well: David's Story. Mildred D. Taylor. New York: Dial Books for Young Readers, 1995. *74*

Index of Authors

Index of Books by Reading Level

The Givens Foundation for African American Literature

The Givens Foundation for African American Literature was established in 1972 as the Archie and Phebe Mae Givens Foundation. Its original purpose was to provide scholarships to African American students. The Foundation's focus shifted in 1985 when the Givens family worked with the Twin Cities African American community to purchase a 3,000-piece collection of African American literature—one of the most important collections of its kind in the nation. Since then, the Archie Givens Sr. Collection of African American Literature housed at the University of Minnesota Library has inspired and supported the Foundation's efforts.

Today, the mission of the Foundation is to celebrate and promote African American literature and history through programs and activities that encourage reading and increase public awareness of African American writers. The Foundation is guided by a volunteer advisory board. *Spirited Minds: African American Books for Our Sons and Our Brothers* is the first major publication of the Foundation.

Archie Givens is Director of the Givens Foundation for African American Literature.